Argentina

Argentina

BY MARTIN HINTZ

Enchantment of the World
Second Series

Children's Press®

A Division of Grolier Publishing

NEW YORK   LONDON   HONG KONG   SYDNEY
DANBURY, CONNECTICUT

To the *Desaparecidos* (the Disappeared):
Beatriz Hernandez Hobbas,
Washington Fernando Hernandez Hobbas,
and the more than 250 other children who disappeared
during the "Dirty War" between 1976 and 1983

Consultant: James Cockcroft, Professor, Ramapo College

Please note: All statistics are as up-to-date as possible at the time of publication.

Visit Children's Press on the Internet: http://publishing.grolier.com

Book production by Editorial Directions, Inc.
Book design by Ox and Company, Inc.

Library of Congress Cataloging-in-Publication Data

Hintz, Martin.
        Argentina / by Martin Hintz.
        cm. — (Enchantment of the world. Second series)
        Includes bibliographical references (p.   ) and index.
Summary: Describes the geography, history, culture, religion, and people of the environmentally diverse South American country of Argentina.
        ISBN 0-516-20647-8
        Argentina — Juvenile literature. [1. Argentina.] I. Title. II. Series
        F2808.2.H56 1998
        982–dc21   97-40666
                                                   CIP
                                                   AC

Acknowledgments

For assistance in this book, the author wishes to thank the Argentine Embassy and Consulate, as well as the Argentine ministries of economics, press relations and culture, education, and interior.

Contents

Cover photo:
Fishing village

Iguaçú Falls

Seal pups

Buenos Días, Argentina

Argentina is one of the most sophisticated countries in South America and one of the most fascinating. Its landscape is as rich and varied as its people. Many nationalities and many cultures mix in Argentina and each group adds to its charm.

Argentina is rich in agricultural resources.

ARGENTINA IS ALSO RICH IN NATURAL RESOURCES. AGRICULture is a strong industry and manufacturing is on the rise. Tourism and mining are also important to the nation's economy.

A Marvelous Mix

Argentina's landscape ranges from the broad plains of the Pampa to towering mountains and vast deserts, from waterfalls and prairies to rushing rivers, wide lakes, and icebergs. This is a land of contrasts, which makes it sometimes difficult to live in.

Argentines must deal with the harsh winters of the Andes, fierce storms on the Atlantic Ocean, and howling winds on the dusty Pampa. Such challenges make the Argentines a strong and flexible people. Whatever Mother Nature cares to toss at them, they'll handle it.

Argentina's Capital City

Buenos Aires, Argentina's capital, is one of the world's largest cities. Because of its size, the 12 million residents of its metropolitan area have to put up with some irritants. The city has occasional power outages, and heavy rainfall may plug the storm drains. Air pollution and traffic congestion are also problems. But the city has no decaying downtown or sprawling slums.

Opposite: **Open-air tango musicians**

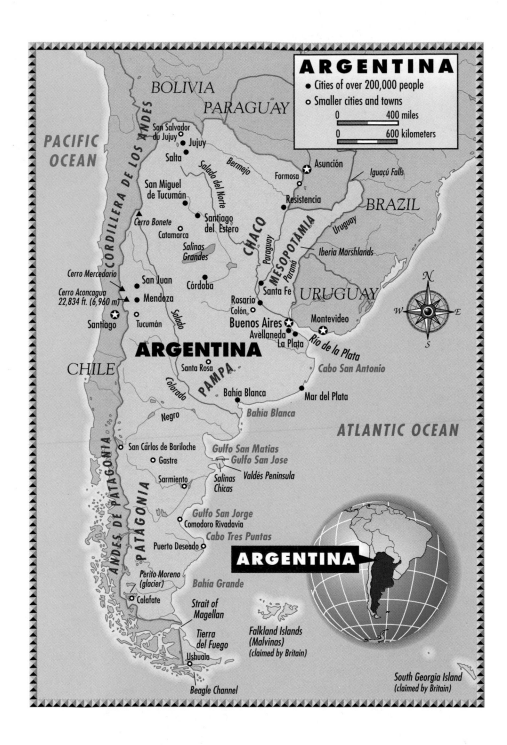

ARGENTINA

- Cities of over 200,000 people
- Smaller cities and towns

0 ——— 400 miles
0 ——— 600 kilometers

BOLIVIA

PARAGUAY

PACIFIC OCEAN

San Salvador du Jujuy
Jujuy
Salta
Bermejo
Asunción
Formosa
Iguaçú Falls

CORDILLERA DE LOS ANDES

San Miguel de Tucumán
Salado del Norte
Resistencia
BRAZIL

Cerro Bonete
Catamarca
Santiago del Estero
CHACO
Uruguay

Salinas Grandes
MESOPOTAMIA
Iberia Marshlands

Cerro Mercedario
San Juan
Córdoba
Paraguay
Paraná
Santa Fe
URUGUAY

Cerro Aconcagua 22,834 ft. (6,960 m)
Mendoza
Rosario
Colón
Montevideo

Santiago
Tucumán
Buenos Aires
Avellaneda
La Plata
Río de la Plata

ARGENTINA

Salado
Santa Rosa
PAMPA
Cabo San Antonio

CHILE
Colorado
Bahía Blanca
Mar del Plata
Bahía Blanca

Negro
ATLANTIC OCEAN

San Carlos de Bariloche
Gastre
Gulfo San Matias
Gulfo San Jose

ANDES DE PATAGONIA
Sarmiento
Salinas Chicas
Valdés Peninsula

PATAGONIA
Gulfo San Jorge
Comodoro Rivadavia
Cabo Tres Puntas

Puerto Deseado

ARGENTINA

Perito Moreno (glacier)
Bahía Grande
Calafate

Strait of Magellan
Falkland Islands (Malvinas) (claimed by Britain)

Tierra del Fuego
Ushuaia

Beagle Channel

South Georgia Island (claimed by Britain)

Geopolitical map of Argentina

Buenos Aires is a cosmopolitan city with tree-shaded parks, wide boulevards, and an interesting mix of architecture. This is a city that never sleeps. People are out on the streets at 2 A.M., on their way to a dance club, a restaurant, or a late show. The pace of life is fast. Everyone seems to be on an important errand. It is the place to make deals—big deals. Thousands of Argentines have left their rural communities and flocked to Buenos Aires and other cities. They want a piece of the action, too.

If there are any intra-Argentine differences, they are most obvious between city dwellers and people who still live in the countryside. Today, more than eight out of ten of Argentines live in cities or large towns and more than one-third of the entire population lives in the capital or its suburbs. Buenos Aires residents feel that their hometown is the best anywhere—and the most important too. They tend to look down their noses at Argentines who live elsewhere.

A Split in Society

Naturally, people who live in smaller towns and on farms don't like that attitude. Hard feelings between Buenos Aires and the rest of the country have often led to political unrest, when the city dwellers battled the rich landowners during the period before Argentina became independent.

Argentine society has been influenced by this history. As the port cities grew rich and strong, the poorer people flocked from the provinces to the coast to find work. They often had trouble finding good jobs because they were unskilled. The

unemployed were called "the shirtless ones" and they tended to support anyone who promised them a better life, even dictators.

The upper and middle classes in the cities resented these newcomers and distrusted the politicians who catered to them. The military then felt they could do a better job than the quarreling civilians, so they stepped in to run things.

Argentine families throughout society are close-knit, however. Families are extremely important and loyalty is seen as a great virtue. Family connections are often necessary to get a decent job, or even to get into a good school. And the family is always there to help.

Political demonstrations are not uncommon in Argentina.

Opposite: **Perito Moreno Glacier in Patagonia**

Strength and Weakness

Family feeling is both a strength and a weakness for Argentina. Too much dependence can restrict one's growth but it also makes for a powerful force that can stand up to trouble.

So that's Argentina. Confusing, perhaps, at first glance. But on closer inspection, it is an enchanting nation.

The Tail of South America

Argentina forms the "tail" of South America. It is the eighth-largest nation in the world and the second-largest in South America, after Brazil. Shaped like a blunted wedge, Argentina is 980 miles (1,577 km) wide and stretches 2,300 miles (3,700 km) from its northern borders to the skinny tip of Tierra del Fuego in the far south.

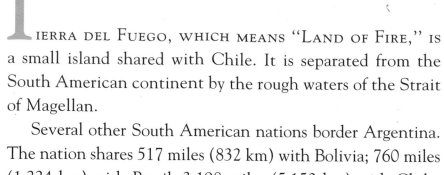

TIERRA DEL FUEGO, WHICH MEANS "LAND OF FIRE," IS a small island shared with Chile. It is separated from the South American continent by the rough waters of the Strait of Magellan.

Several other South American nations border Argentina. The nation shares 517 miles (832 km) with Bolivia; 760 miles (1,224 km) with Brazil; 3,198 miles (5,150 km) with Chile; 1,167 miles (1,880 km) with Paraguay; and 360 miles (579 km) with Uruguay. The Atlantic Ocean forms the eastern border, with 2,936 miles (4,725 km) of coastline. Argentina's exact size is sometimes open to question because of frontier disputes with its neighbors, especially Uruguay and Chile. And despite losing a war with Great Britain in 1982, Argentina still claims the British-administered Falkland Islands (Islas Malvinas).

A sea lion colony

Rich Diversity

Argentina's area covers 1,073,400 square miles (2,780,092 sq km) in a rich mix of lush grasslands and thick forests. It is about three-tenths the size of the United States, not including another vast piece of territory that Argentina also claims. That territory consists of 374,300 frostbitten square miles (969,432 sq km) in Antarctica.

Its length and the variety of its landscape make Argentina one of the most fascinating countries in the world. It has

Lake Nahuel Huapí in the Andean lake district

deserts, mountains, seacoasts, broad plains, and rolling hills. Few countries can match Argentina's diversity.

One of the country's interesting natural phenomena is Perito Moreno, the only inland glacier in the world that is still growing. It is located in Patagonia, near the village of Calafate. The huge ice sheet moves forward 30 feet (9 m) each year, which is speedy for glaciers. The river of shimmering blue ice is near two lakes: Largo Argentino and Brazo Rico. The blue color comes from the oxygen that is trapped in the ice when it falls as snow. The lakes are separated by a barrier of ice that dams the waters of the Brazo Rico. Every five years or so, however, the pressure of the water breaks the ice wall and the torrent rushes into Lago Argentino. The height of that lake then rises an astonishing 102 feet (31 m) in a matter of minutes.

Great Distances

To get an idea of the great distances in Argentina, take a train trip from Buenos Aires to the town of San Salvador de Jujuy in northwest Argentina—a journey of 1,000 miles (1,609 km). From Buenos Aires south, you can travel by train to the port of Río Gallegos, almost 1,600 miles (2,574 km) away at the southern tip of the country.

Many Rivers, Many Mountains

Argentina's many rivers provide water for agricultural irrigation. The northeast is drained by the Paraguay and Paraná Rivers, which rise in Argentina's central plateau. The Uruguay River, also in the northeast, forms Argentina's border with Uruguay and Brazil. These three north–south waterways and their major tributaries (the Pilcomayo, Bermejo, and Salado) rush down from the Andes and empty into Río de la Plata.

Perito Moreno is the fastest-moving glacier in the world.

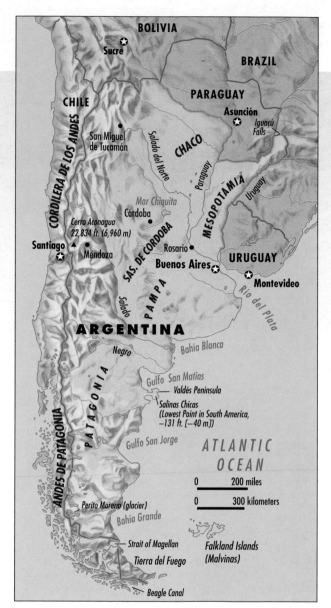

Geographical Features

Highest Elevation: Aconcagua, 22,834 feet (6,960 m) above sea level

Lowest Elevation: Valdés Peninsula, 131 feet (40 m) below sea level

Largest City: Buenos Aires

Highest Average Temperature: In northern Argentina: January, 80°F (27°C); August, 60°F (16°C)

Lowest Average Temperature: In southern Argentina: January, 60°F (16°C); August, 32°F (0°C)

Longest River: Río de la Plata drains an area of 1.6 million square miles (4.1 million sq km)

Widest Lake: Lake Colhué Huapí, 3,031 square miles (7,850 sq km)

The estuary—the river's wide mouth—lies between Argentina and Uruguay. The major rivers in central and southern Argentina—the Colorado, Negro, Chubut, Deseado, Chico, and Santa Cruz—originate in the Andes. The mud-brown Colorado is the nation's second-largest river, at 744 miles (1,197 km) long, after the Río de la Plata.

Argentina is easily divided into three major sections. First, there is the Pampa, an area of flat, fertile plains in the east central section that covers more than 250,959 square miles (650,000 sq km). The soil in the Pampa consists of fine sand, clay, and dirt washed eastward by the fierce winds and driving rains that regularly sweep over the

The Santa Cruz River

land. Nothing rises up on this vast plain, except some low hills near Mar del Plata on the Atlantic Coast and some ancient

Gauchos still herd cattle on the Pampa.

mountains in central Argentina. The Pampa is now crisscrossed by railroad tracks and highways, but in the past, it was a lot like the shoot-'em-up Wild West in the United States. Thousands of cattle once roamed the open range, herded by *gauchos*— the hard-riding South American cowboys who became folk heroes.

The mighty Andes make travel difficult in winter months.

Rugged Andes

Another distinguishing feature of Argentina is the rugged Andes Mountains on its western border. These lofty mountains, which run like a rocky spine down the length of South America, include the highest mountain in the Western Hemisphere. This is Mount Aconcagua, at 22,834 feet (6,960 m). Other towering peaks are Bonete, at 22,546 feet (6,872 m) and Mercedario, at 22,211 feet (6,770 m). Wide valleys, called *quebradas*, run through the Andes. Since the days of Spanish rule, the quebradas have been used for transportation. The Uspallata Pass, at 12,600 feet (3,840 m) is one of the main routes to Chile. The magnificent Christ of the Andes statue stands at the pass. It was built in 1904 to commemorate a boundary settlement between Chile and Argentina. Early explorers called this pass *Camino de los Andes* (Road of the Andes).

The Rose of the Incas

The Rose of the Incas (manganese spar) is Argentina's national stone. It is often made into beautiful jewelry, with some of the best examples of local craftwork found in Catamarca, a village in the high northwest.

During South America's revolutionary days, armies marched back and forth along the Camino de los Andes. Now a railroad makes travel easier—and safer. Small planes sometimes fly through the pass to avoid the higher peaks of the Andes. But travel here is never easy. In winter, blinding snowstorms rage between the valley walls, and the mountain passes are often blocked by deep drifts.

Rolling Hills

South and east of the Andes, rolling hills blend into broad plains that extend to the Atlantic. This is Patagonia, which makes up about 25 percent of Argentina's land. In spring, Patagonia is crisscrossed by deep canyons full of muddy, rushing water. While the land is not suitable for extensive farming it is fine for sheep raising. Only cacti and stunted trees dot this desolate landscape.

Between 1910 and 1921, the government built irrigation canals along the Río Negro in Patagonia for the development of orchards and vineyards. Today, thousands of tons of grapes and other fruit are produced here.

Rivers and streams cut many valleys into the dry land of Patagonia.

Environmental Issues

Argentina must deal with many environmental problems, some caused by nature and some by people. The country has erosion problems resulting from inadequate flood control and improper land use. Overuse of irrigation for farming affects the underground water table in some areas. Buenos Aires has a major air-pollution problem, resulting mainly from motor vehicle emissions. Some major cities have water-pollution problems and rivers are also becoming polluted because of runoff from pesticides and fertilizers.

The government is working to correct many of these problems. Argentina has signed international treaties that deal with such global issues as disposal of hazardous wastes, ocean dumping, and nuclear tests, and set up laws to protect the ozone layer and the Antarctic.

But no one can do much about natural hazards. Earthquakes rumble regularly in the Tucumán and Mendoza areas of the Andes. Argentina also has to deal with heavy flooding after rains, snowstorms in the mountains, and windstorms across the Pampa.

Wide Plains and Waterfalls

Two major geographical sections of northern Argentina are the Chaco and Mesopotamia. The Chaco's broad plain extends into Paraguay, western Brazil, and eastern Bolivia. Many rivers meander across the landscape, including the Paraná and Uruguay. People who live near the water build their houses on log pilings or high earthen embankments as protection against raging floods. However, the Chaco's warm, moist climate makes it excellent for farming.

Mesopotamia lies just east of the Andes. It was named after an ancient land called Mesopotamia because it reminded early settlers of that fertile region. Rainfall is plentiful in Mesopotamia, too, making it a fine agricultural region. Many reed-choked swamps and muggy tropical jungles add variety to its landscape.

The Iguaçú River, which Argentina shares with Brazil, tumbles into Iguaçú Falls, a waterfall that is larger than Niagara Falls in North America. *Iguaçú* means "great waters" in the Guaraní language. For about 3 miles (5 km), the Paraná River roars over jagged rocks. It then tumbles over a cliff that is 8,100 feet (2,469 m) wide with drops of more than 200 feet (61 m). Visitors to Iguaçú National

Park can get a close look at the falls by inching along a catwalk on the river's edge. The waterfall was featured in the British movie *The Mission* (1986). Today, a huge hydroelectric power plant straddles the waterway upriver from the falls.

Temperate Climate

Argentina's climate depends mainly on location, ranging from extreme heat in the Chaco region to mild temperatures in the central Pampa and mild to cold in southern Patagonia. Remember that the seasons here are the opposite of seasons in

Cattle in the Chaco region near Paraguay

Iguaçú Falls in Iguaçú National Park

Looking at Argentina's Cities

also an Argentine naval base and several multinational companies, such as Germany's Grundig and Japan's Sansui, that produce television sets and other electronic equipment. Sheep ranchers of Scottish descent work in the countryside and many residents of Italian descent live in the community. The *Museo Territorial* (The Museum at the End of the Earth) has artifacts covering the town's history. Five ski centers are nearby. The average January temperature is 50°F (10°C); the average July temperature is 34°F (1°C). At noon in wintry June and July, the sun barely rises above the horizon.

San Carlos de Bariloche, or Bariloche for short, is the country's chief ski resort (below). It lies in the center of the Argentine lake district in Patagonia and has many shops

Ushuaia (above), the southernmost town in South America, lies at the tip of Tierra del Fuego, the "Land of Fire." The site was named by sailors aboard the ship of explorer Ferdinand Magellan in 1520, when they saw fires on the land. The fires had been lit by local Native Americans—the Ona, Haupí, Yamana, Alacaluf, and Yaghan.

English and Italian missionaries settled here in the 1880s and a prison was built in town in 1896. There is

catering to downhill and cross-country skiers. The town stands along the shore of glacial Lago Colhué Huapí. In winter, the snow reaches the rooftops of houses in the nearby mountains. The population consists of Argentines of Spanish, German, Swiss, and Italian heritage. The average January temperature here is 64°F (18°C); the average July temperature is 36°F (2°C).

Salta is a Native American word meaning "place of stones." It is also the name of the capital of Jujuy province in Argentina's far northwest. Located on a high, cold Andean plateau, Salta has been an important agricultural town since its founding by the Spanish in 1582. Its position on the overland route from Buenos Aires to Lima, Peru, made it an important city and the colonial look of its buildings (opposite, lower left) makes it an important historic site. The average January temperature is 60°F (16°C); the average July temperature is 45°F (7°C).

Posadas is the capital of Misiones province, at the northeast tip of Argentina. The area got its name from a string of Jesuit missions (right, in ruins) established throughout the area in the 1500s. Many of the old families here are of Native American heritage. After the Spanish, Poles, and Ukrainians arrived as early as 1890 they were followed by English, Swiss, Brazilians, Swedes, Germans, and Japanese. The surrounding area is important for the logging industry, as well as for farming. The average January temperature is 83°F (28°C); the average July temperature is 56°F (13°C).

Zondas are common in the cactus-filled western plateau.

the Northern Hemisphere. When it is winter in the United States and Canada, it is summer in Argentina. Since Argentina is close to the Atlantic Ocean, seasonal changes are fairly moderate. Extreme temperature changes like those in North America occur in the far northwest, in the Andes.

Argentina's great north–south distance also affects the climate. In the northwest, the towering Andean peaks are only covered with snow at 20,000 feet (6,100 m). At the southern tip of the country, the snow line is below 1,500 feet (457 m).

Moist winds rise up from the Pacific Ocean on the west, bringing rain and snow to the highest slopes of the Andes. As these prevailing westerly winds descend on the eastern slopes of the Andes, they become warmer and increase their ability to absorb moisture. As a result, few clouds form and rainfall is minimal throughout Argentina's hot, dry western plateau. These dust-filled winds are called *zondas*.

In addition to zondas, a cold offshore current in the Atlantic contributes to the dry climate. Moist air cools over the ocean and loses its moisture in the form of fog or rain before it moves inland. As a result, much of the coastline gets heavy fogs early in the day. On the Atlantic coast, Patagonia is very dry. More than two-thirds of Argentina does not receive enough rain for extensive agriculture, so fields must be irrigated. However, *sudestada*—storms off the Atlantic Ocean—bring heavy rains that create flash floods along the dry riverbeds. In some of the driest areas, dust storms roar across the plains. Powerful storms called *pamperos* occasionally sweep up from the south, bringing cold and snow to Buenos Aires.

Increased Precipitation

In the extreme south, precipitation increases because the Andes are lower, allowing the moisture-heavy winds to drift down the slopes. The climate stays cool and moist throughout much of the year, which is ideal for the region's heavy forests.

Tall tales about the nation's weather and landscape are often heard in Argentina. For instance, it is said that the wind on the Pampa is so strong that you should never fire a bullet into the air. Allegedly, the bullet will immediately come back and strike the shooter. It is true, however, that flocks of geese who try to fly into the Argentine wind are often blown backward.

In any case, travel is never boring in Argentina. There is always something different over that vast horizon.

The Ozone Layer and Skin Cancer

A large hole in Earth's ozone layer was found in the atmosphere over South America in May 1997. The ozone layer in the atmosphere protects the Earth from ultraviolet radiation. The hole in the ozone layer stretched from Santiago de Chile on the Pacific Coast to Buenos Aires. It was the first time that the hole had extended so far north.

Authorities in Argentina, however, did not warn people to take precautions against increased sun exposure. The country's weather bureau decided that the matter was of interest only to scientists and that no one else should be concerned.

Since the hole was first observed over South America in the early 1980s, deaths in Argentina from skin cancer have increased 127 percent. Some of this increase could be attributed to the increased ultraviolet rays, according to the scientists.

Plants and Animals

Like Argentina's landscape, the country's vegetation seems to be different at every turn. It ranges from the great stretch of rain forests in the northern province of Misiones to the lichen-covered rocks on the far southern islands.

L ET'S TAKE A STEP BACK IN HISTORY. About 150 million years ago, a large forest of araucaria trees stood on the outskirts of Sarmiento, about 99 miles (160 km) west of Comodoro Rivadavia in Chubut province. Lava and ash from nearby volcanic eruptions buried that forest, and, over time, the giant trees became fossilized. Through the centuries, wind and water swept away the soil, leaving a spooky landscape of petrified tree trunks up to 28 feet (8.5 m) high and 2 feet (60 cm) in diameter.

A large petrified log in the Petrified National Park

Today's Vegetation

Now let's move ahead to today's Argentina, where thousands of plant species are alive and well. The soil and climate in any locale determine what grows best there. In the high, dry Andes, nothing grows but scruffy ichu grass and some hardy evergreen shrubs. However, rainfall along the eastern edges of the mountains and in the foothills allows taller trees to grow.

Opposite: **Lichen-covered rocks along a stream in Tierra del Fuego National Park**

The red earth of northern Argentina

The palm savannas are found in the hot, dry Chaco where thorn thickets are so dense that they are difficult to chop through. Pine forests range along the fog-bound Atlantic Coast. The southern plateaus are the grassy home of fat, contented sheep, while thick tropical jungles and swamps cover much of Mesopotamia.

Look carefully at the different soils in the northeast and the Pampa, Argentina's major agricultural areas. The Pampa has a healthy, protective layer of organic matter at its surface and a deep, fertile subsoil called chernozem. This combination is so soft and rich that alfalfa roots can penetrate 15 feet (6 m) into it. But in northeastern Argentina, the deep red soil comes from pulverized volcanic rocks, which is especially evident on the Paraná Plateau in Misiones province. This red earth looks like many soils throughout the tropics, but it is quite different. Argentina's red soil has plant nutrients and is well drained. Subsequently, citrus fruit, sugarcane, and maté flourish there. Sometimes fertilizer is used to give it an extra growth kick.

The climate also affects vegetation. For instance, the Pampa is divided into two weather zones that greatly affect what grows there. The Pampa *húmeda*, Argentina's main grain and livestock area, gets plenty of rain. The Pampa *seca* is drier, so its crops have to be irrigated.

Argentina has some plant varieties found nowhere else in the world. An interesting tree called the *quebracho* grows in the Chaco. It is also known as the "ax-breaker" because its wood is so hard. The quebracho is used for railroad ties, fence posts, and telephone poles. It is also a source of tannin, a substance used in tanning leather. Unfortunately, over the years, woodcutters have devastated the quebracho forests. It takes more than 100 years for a quebracho to mature, so these trees are increasingly rare. Cotton is now grown where the trees used to stand.

A door made from the quebracho tree

Argentina is one of the world's major exporters of agricultural products. Wheat is the chief crop, especially in the Pampa, taking up about one-seventh of the nation's cropland. Maize (corn) also has high yields. Flax is grown for linseed oil; rye, barley, and oats are used for animal feed; and sunflower seeds are a primary source for cooking oil. Before the harvest, vast fields of bright yellow sunflowers roll across the plains in

Yerba Maté

Yerba maté, Argentina's favorite drink, is made from a small tree of the same name. Yerba maté is also known as Paraguayan tea. The tree, native to South America, is found along the borders Argentina shares with Paraguay and Brazil. Its leaves are dried, roasted, crushed, and then submerged in boiling water to prepare for drinking. The Guaraní, who believed the tea had medicinal powers, taught the Spanish how to make it. The Guaraní put dried leaves in a gourd (also called a *maté*) filled with hot water. The tea could then be sipped through a reed tube. The early Spanish added a European touch by drinking from a maté made of wood or silver and using a silver *bombilla* (little pump) with a gold-plated mouthpiece instead of a reed.

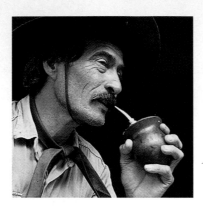

The tea became a favorite of the gauchos, Argentina's cowboys. They always carried a small pouch of leaves on their cattle-herding chores for a quick pick-me-up drink. The Jesuit missions in Misiones cultivated the plant and it became the province's most important export. When the missions were destroyed, imports from Paraguay and Brazil were needed to meet the demand. In the early 1900s, Argentina reestablished its yerba maté plantations (*yerbales*) in the provinces of Misiones, Corrientes, and the Chaco.

Mixed with aromatic herbs and cold water, the drink is called *tereré*. A *rueda de maté* (a maté round) is a kind of tea party. Shoppers can also purchase maté bags. To cut the bitter taste, many Argentines add lots of sugar.

a mighty, wind-swept carpet of color. Near Tucumán in the northwest, sugarcane grows well. Vineyards and orchards produce tons of sweet grapes, apples, pears, and other fruits. Sorghum, soybeans, and sugar beets also contribute to the farm economy.

Ancient Animals and National Parks

Millions of years ago, the Valle de la Luna (Valley of the Moon) in the far northwest province of San Juan was once a lake bed. Today, scientists in that area unearth fossils of dinosaurs and other creatures, as well as of ancient plants.

After the dinosaurs, huge elephant-like beasts with stubby trunks lived in the valley as did penguins that stood taller than a man. Doglike animals that were as large as wolves were really marsupials—animals that carry their young in a pouch on their belly like kangaroos.

Today, Argentina has set aside thirteen national parks in an effort to preserve what remains of the country's native animal life. Urban sprawl and agriculture have taken up much of the animals' natural habitat. While all the parks have a wide range of plants, birds, and animals, some species are limited to one or two of these sites. The national park near Iguaçú Falls protects 2,000 species of plant life and some 400 kinds of birds, such as the yellow-beaked toucan and multicolored *colibrí* (hummingbird). Flocks of butterflies waft among the trees like tattered rainbows. A wide range of other animals

A jaguar hiding in lush vegetation

roam the park, including jaguars and *yacarés* (alligators), whose yawning grins show off razor-sharp teeth. Chattering monkeys scamper among the treetops while wild hogs crash through the thick undergrowth.

Living Tank

The *tatú carreta*, a giant armadillo-like creature that is built like a living tank, has a haven in Formosa Nature Reserve, which lies between the Teuco and Teuquito Rivers. Red foxes, guanacos, beavers, and ducks are safe within the borders of Tierra del Fuego National Park at the southern tip of Argentina. Overhead, majestic condors soar with wingspreads of 10 feet (3 m). At Ría del Deseado Nature Reserve, on the Atlantic Coast, ravens, gulls, and Antarctic doves swoop over sea lions basking on the rocks.

Ancient trees in El Palmar National Park

Several exotic types of plant life can be seen in national parks. The last examples of the sprawling Yatay palm trees are found in El Palmar National Park, 31 miles (50 km) north of Colón. Some of the trees are thought to be 800 years old. In the Patagonian Andes, Arraynes National Park includes a forest with 1,000-year-old arrayán trees. The ancient arrayán—a bushy tree with a smooth, cinnamon-colored bark—grows in dense groves where only a little sunlight can filter through. According to local lore, moviemaker Walt Disney supposedly got his inspiration here for the film about Bambi the deer.

By the end of the twentieth century, Los Cardones National Park will be added to the list of protected areas. The park, in the northwest Calchaquíes Valley, is named after a towering cactus. Ancient tribes used the sturdy cactus to build their homes.

Animals in the Wild

In areas that are not densely populated, wild animals can still roam free. The 270,200 acres (109,000 ha) of the humid Iberá marshlands are home to swamp deer, turtles, alligators, monkeys, and capybaras, the world's largest rodent. The viscacha is a burrowing rodent that looks like a North American prairie dog while the zorillo is a skunk with a nose like a pig's snout. One of the most interesting Argentine animals is the rhea, a three-toed bird that looks like an ostrich and grows up to 6 feet (2 m) tall. Some ranches allow children to ride on the backs of these giant birds. Sure-footed mountain sheep eat and live on the heights of the Andes.

Llama and Alpaca

The llama that lives in Argentina's mountains is a member of the camel family. Camels are native to North America, evolving more than 45 million years ago. Some 3 million years ago, they migrated into Asia and South America. The vicuña, guanaco, and alpaca are also related animals, or cameloids. Well adapted to life in the high Andes, they have soft pads on their feet to help them get across the rocks and shaggy coats to protect them from the cold. The guanaco does not need to drink water. It gets all the moisture it needs from its food.

The llama and alpaca were tamed by Native Americans at least 4,000 years ago and used as beasts of burden like horses or oxen. Their thick wool makes excellent sweaters and ponchos (capes). The guanaco and vicuña are often killed by gauchos for food.

The viscacha are members of the rodent family.

In rural Patagonia, a careful observer may spot the rare Patagonian gray fox and the mouse-sized opossum. The Patagonian hare, the mara, is about 30 inches long (76 cm). This rabbitlike animal has short ears but longer legs than its North American cousin. Numerous exotic birds are natives of Patagonia, including the tufted tit-tyrant, the crested tinamou, herons, parrots, and the red-backed hawk. More than 50,000 migrating birds, including the Puna duck and two species of flamingo, come to Laguna de los Pozuelos. The shallow waters of the lake and surrounding marshland sit on a high plateau above the city of Jujuy.

Argentina has a number of poisonous snakes, such as rattlers, coral snakes, and cruz snakes, but they generally do not bother anyone unless they feel threatened. Sometimes, farm fields are devastated by locusts—insects that swarm up from the southern Chaco and devour everything green.

The waters of Argentina are rich in marine life. With their plentiful trout and bass, the country's lakes and rivers are a paradise for anglers. The dorado, a dolphin, weighs up to 77 pounds (35 kg). Every year, the Anglers National Dorado Fishing Contest is held in Formosa. But even the dorado seems small compared with the manguruyú, which reaches 220 pounds (100 kg), and the surubí, peaking out at 132 pounds (60 kg). Shellfish, sea snails, and conch are sold commercially. Large sharks are caught regularly in the Atlantic

Ocean and killer whales traveling in packs attack schools of fish. Sea lions bob about in offshore waters. Off the southern coast, more than 1 million Magellan penguins gather at the Punta Tombo Reserve from mid-September through January. The reserve, one of the most varied seabird colonies in the world, has the largest number of penguins outside Antarctica.

Roaring bull sea lions stake out their turf on the rocks of Punta Pirámide while three species of cormorants—a diving, fish-eating bird—zoom above. Whales come to breed in the frigid, black waters of the Nuevo and San José Gulfs that link the islands and the mainland. Scientists have worked in the area for so long that they have named individual whales and know if they return every year. Like massive torpedoes, the whales actually leap almost clear of the water. Their enormous tails give them the strength to put on this amazing show.

Sea lion pups bark to their mothers.

Argentina is famous for its fine horses.

Animals on the Ranch

Argentina's farm animals are similar to those found elsewhere in the world. Goats, pigs, poultry, and cattle—you name it and the Argentines have it. The people may tolerate these animals as necessary for food, but they take pride in their horses. Horses were brought to South America by the Spanish in the 1500s. Some escaped and others were turned loose. Within decades, great herds of wild horses thundered across the Pampa. They were hunted for their hides and tallow by the *mestizo*, or mixed-race, gauchos, who were also great horsemen. Native Americans who captured and trained the horses became superb riders and warriors. These skilled horsemen roamed at will across the landscape, preventing European settlement. The great *estancias*, or horse ranches, were not established until the end of the 1800s.

Cattle on the Pampa

Río Gallegos, which flows for 180 miles (290 km) along the Patagonia Atlantic coast is the center for sheep raising in southern Argentina. It is said that there are more than 100 sheep for every person in some remote parts of Argentina. Basques from Spain, Scots, and Welsh people came to Argentina to tend the hardy flocks whose dense, valuable coats protect them from the harsh weather.

Cattle roam the broad Pampa. They are not as free as they were in the days before railroads, highways, and fences broke up the landscape, but they are still out there, grazing on sprawling ranches that seem as big as Texas. Aberdeen Angus, shorthorn, Hereford, and Charolais are favorites for meat production. Holando Argentino cows are fine milk producers. Argentina has a fabulous variety of flora and fauna, of plants and animals. Its amazing wildlife help to make this country great.

Tumultuous History

Native Americans were living in Argentina for thousands of years before the first Europeans arrived. At least twenty major tribes and numerous clans lived in the Pampa, the mountains, and along the seashores. Some were nomads who lived by hunting. They chased herds of deer for days if need be, without letting the animals eat or drink. Eventually, the deer became so exhausted that they were easily killed by arrows and slingshots.

Meeting the People

OTHER NATIVE AMERICANS WERE FARMERS. They lived in walled villages and developed a widespread trading system throughout South America. Instead of growing wheat, tribes such as the Querandi made a flour mash of crushed and roasted locusts.

In 1520, the explorer Ferdinand Magellan met Native Americans at the tip of South America. He thought they had very large feet, and he wrote long stories about the giants in the terrible lands of Patagonia. Though these people were taller than most Spaniards, they were not giants. However, they were frightening to look at from a European point of view. They hunted seal, alpaca, guanaco, and rhea. Later explorers realized that these hardy people would not attack them.

The European invaders were not impressed with the other Native Americans they encountered when they arrived in 1516.

Ferdinand Magellan

Opposite: **A Tehuelche woman**

Boleadoras

A favorite Indian weapon was the boleadoras. It consisted of two or three stones tied together by leather thongs and could be thrown accurately up to 100 yards (91 m). The boleadoras wrapped around the legs of an animal and brought it down.

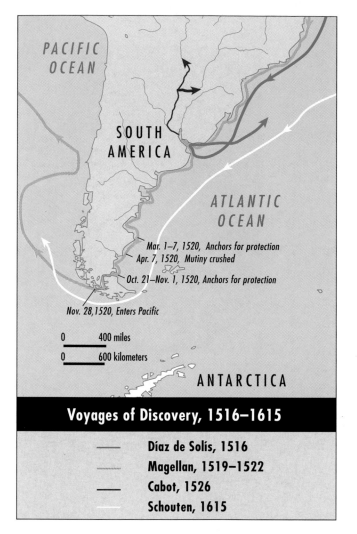

PACIFIC
OCEAN

SOUTH
AMERICA

ATLANTIC
OCEAN

Mar. 1–7, 1520, Anchors for protection
Apr. 7, 1520, Mutiny crushed
Oct. 21–Nov. 1, 1520, Anchors for protection

Nov. 28, 1520, Enters Pacific

0   400 miles
0   600 kilometers

ANTARCTICA

Voyages of Discovery, 1516–1615

—— **Díaz de Solís, 1516**
—— **Magellan, 1519–1522**
—— **Cabot, 1526**
—— **Schouten, 1615**

The Indians dressed in skins and furs and they ate animal fat. According to the Spanish, this proved the Native Americans were nothing but savages and "grease eaters." The first Spaniard to land in what is now Argentina was Juan Díaz de Solís. The king of Spain had sent him to find a passage to the Pacific Ocean around South America. Díaz de Solís found the mouth of the Río de la Plata (the River of Silver). But in 1516, only grassy plains edged its shores. Díaz de Solís decided to go farther upstream.

Invited to Dinner

Taking a group of hard-bitten soldiers and sailors from his ship, Díaz de Solís rowed ashore in a small boat. He saw some Native Americans who looked friendly and who invited the Spaniards to dinner. The Spaniards didn't realize that they were to be the main course! The unfortunate explorers were eaten. But some of the men escaped back to Spain with pieces of silver they had found. This news launched a silver rush to Argentina.

In fact, the word *argentina* means "silver" or "silvery" in Spanish. It comes from the Latin term for silver, *argentum*.

Thus the nation of Argentina is the "Silver Country."

But the fortune hunters were disappointed and soon gave up when they found very little silver. For many years afterward, it was easier to cross the Andes from the Bolivian and the Chilean side of the mountains where the Native Americans had their silver mines. The Spanish tried to establish a trade route from Buenos Aires to the mines in Bolivia but this venture was plagued by flooding during the wet season in the Chaco as well as by hostile tribes.

The first colonizers tried to make laborers out of the free-spirited Guaraní, Huarpe, Comechingone, and other Native Americans. That was a big mistake. The Europeans did not understand how much these people valued their freedom. In addition, when the Araucanians invaded Argentina from Chile, the Spaniards were not prepared. Bands of 200 to 300 mounted Indians swooped down on Spanish settlements and missions and burned them out. Many of the early Argentine towns were destroyed in these raids. Even Buenos Aires was abandoned because the colonizers feared attacks. It was not until 1580 that the area around the city was considered safe enough for the Spaniards to return.

Native Americans working in deep silver mines

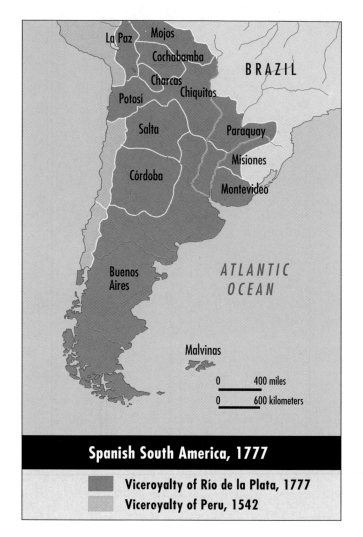

Spanish South America, 1777

Viceroyalty of Río de la Plata, 1777
Viceroyalty of Peru, 1542

Spanish Settlers

In the 1600s and early 1700s, the Spanish concentrated on colonizing Bolivia, Peru, and Mexico. Nobody thought much about what was going on in Argentina, except traders who wanted to keep the roads open. Villages such as Sante Fe, Córdoba, Catamarca, Santiago del Estero, Tucumán, Salta, and Jujuy become prosperous. They were centers where mule trains could stop for supplies on their long journey from the interior to the coast. However, their distance from the major Spanish fortresses elsewhere in South America contributed to the independent spirit of the few Spaniards who settled the Argentine frontier. Many of the first settlers earned a good living by smuggling. They were so far away that the Spanish governors, the viceroys, could not control them.

By the late 1700s, the Spanish took a closer look at Argentina and encouraged more direct trade with the colony. The Spaniards subdivided their empire in a vain attempt to protect their interests from the Portuguese in nearby Brazil and from the British. A new viceroyalty of the Río de la Plata was established. Buenos Aires was made its capital.

Reaching for Home Rule

However, the local Spanish residents resented the interference of the Spanish king and of the clerks, judges, and military officers the king sent to run things. The wealthy merchant class and local politicians eyed the success of the American Revolution. They told each other they could do the same thing. The British saw the growing unease in Argentina and took the opportunity to stir up trouble. At that time, Napoléon Bonaparte of France was taking over many European nations and his armies now threatened Spain. In 1806, the British attacked Argentina, confident that Spain was too occupied in Europe to offer much help. They were right.

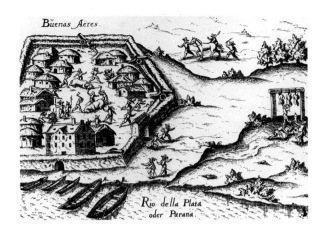

A view of early Buenos Aires

The English attack gained only temporary success.

On June 27, 1806, Buenos Aires was captured by a small group of British troops led by General William Carr Beresford. The city residents didn't like the British any better than the Spanish, however. In August, the townspeople revolted and drove out the British troops. Argentina history books called this the *Reconquista*, which means "take back" or "reconquer." Much later, in one of history's strange twists, the British Embassy in Argentina was located on a Buenos Aires street called the *Calle Reconquista*.

The British launched another attack and retook the city in 1807, but they met the same fate as the first army had and were forced to sign a treaty with Viceroy Santiago Liniers, a Frenchman who had served in the Spanish army. He had been made viceroy in Buenos Aires for his help in defending the city in the first British invasion. This second victory over the British was called the *Defensa*.

More Rebellion

These events showed the Argentines that they could take care of themselves without any help from Spain. This attitude was reinforced in 1808 when France's Napoléon Bonaparte invaded Spain and deposed the Spanish king. Joseph Bonaparte, Napoleon's brother, was installed as ruler. But back in Argentina, the people of Buenos Aires again rebelled. This time, in 1810, it was against the Spanish viceroy sent to replace Liniers. On May 25, 1810, the Argentine upper classes, the Creoles, formed their own government. The Argentines mark the start of their journey to total independence from that day.

Spanish troops were still based on Argentine soil and the Creoles wanted to get them all out of the country. After he had been removed from office in Buenos Aires, former viceroy Liniers had rejoined the Spanish forces. This was unforgivable in the eyes of his old companions who now called themselves the Patriots. Liniers was arrested and executed.

On November 7, 1810, the Patriots defeated a Spanish army at Suipacha and launched the Argentine War of Independence.

Manuel Belgrano and Mariano Moreno were two of the Patriots' best generals, but they had to deal with bitter infighting among the politicians. This caused the Argentines to lose some of their territory to Bolivia. People in the interior also objected to the economic control wielded by the *porteños* (the people of the port) of Buenos Aires. Few people outside the city were given the chance to talk about issues that troubled them or to offer advice on the running of the revolution.

In spite of this turmoil, General José de San Martín, one of the most able of the Patriots' generals, took charge of the situation. In late 1817 and early 1818, he decided to invade Chile, the major Spanish power base. In a great military gamble that paid off, he led his troops over the Andes Mountains through the snowbound Los Patos and Uspallata Passes. Under his leadership, Spain's power in South America was broken.

At this time, Argentina was called the Province of the Río de la Plata. On July 9, 1816, an official proclamation of independence was made. But nobody agreed on how to rule the new country. Should there be a king? A general? An assembly?

Emperor Napoléon Bonaparte

Each provincial city wanted independence from Buenos Aires. Lawlessness was widespread.

In 1820 alone, Buenos Aires had twenty-four governors. Civil war broke out between the *federales*, people from the interior who wished to keep their local power, and the *unitarios*, people who wanted a central government. The election of respected politician Bernardino Rivadavia as governor in 1826 briefly halted the bloodshed. Rivadavia introduced many reforms, but it wasn't enough. Even he was deposed.

Juan Manuel de Rosas became leader of the federales in 1828 and was elected governor in 1829. He was a dictator with a ruthless secret police force and a straightforward way of dealing with his opponents. He killed them. The French and

General José de San Martín

General José de San Martín was born on February 25, 1778, at Yapeyú, a Jesuit mission on the Uruguay River. He went to school in Madrid and he joined the Spanish army at the age of eleven as a cadet. He served in wars in Africa and fought against France's Napoléon Bonaparte, earning the rank of lieutenant colonel. In 1811, after revolution broke out in his homeland of Argentina, he met Francisco de Miranda and other rebel leaders who convinced him to join their cause.

San Martín was a brave soldier who saw the broader picture of

events in South America. He knew the Spanish had to be removed from the continent for his country to be free. San Martín spent two years preparing an army to march across the Andes to successfully attack the Spanish in their Chilean stronghold. But even with his victories in Chile, and ultimately in Bolivia, he stepped aside to let other great revolutionary generals such as Bernardo O'Higgins and Simón Bolívar share the glory. In 1822, he resigned his command and left South America to live in Belgium and France. He died in 1850.

British objected to Rosas's restrictive trade policies, so their combined fleet attacked Buenos Aires in 1848. Although the invaders were driven off, the Argentines had seen enough of Rosas by this time. In 1852, he was replaced by Justo José de Urquiza, one of his former aides, and a constitutional convention met in 1853. The resulting document is still in effect. It granted more power to the Argentine president than the U.S. Constitution grants the U.S. president. One provision allows the president to suspend constitutional guarantees if he considers the country to be "under siege." This means that the president can take over many governmental powers that would ordinarily belong to the Congress or the courts. This clause has been used frequently in Argentine history.

San Martín *(left)* in a painting by Agosto Ballerini

Civil unrest continued under Urquiza's regime. Order was eventually restored after numerous military actions. The next three presidents, General Bartolomé Mitre, Domingo Faustino Sarmiento, and Nicolás Avellaneda favored better education for the people and supported immigration. They had a dark side, though. Under their rule, the rebellious Native Americans were finally subjugated. This was called the Conquest of the Desert, and opened new lands for settlement. But smoldering resentment between the Europeans and Native Americans continued until, over the next forty years, the ancient cultures were finally crushed.

In 1865, Argentina fought a border war with Paraguay. Allied with Brazil and Uruguay in the Triple Alliance, the Argentines defeated the smaller nation. The Paraguayans fought to the death. Almost every adult male in the country was killed.

Roque Sáenz Pena

Only 29,000 men survived the slaughter. However, this war consolidated Argentina's borders. The Pampa was fenced in and industry expanded. The economy boomed, helped in large part by British investments. Soon, the growing middle class demanded more political power.

The *Unión Cívica Radical* (Radical Party) grew strong.

In the old days, only the landowners and other wealthy people could vote. In 1910, Roque Sáenz Pena was inaugurated as president. With his help, Congress passed new voting laws. In 1916, Hipólito Irigoyen was the first Argentine president elected under the reforms. He was not a good leader, though he meant well. He left office in disgrace in 1922. The next president, Marcelo T. de Alvear, did not last long either. In a compromise, the country's political parties agreed to bring Irigoyen back. He was almost eighty years old, but was popular enough to be reelected in 1928.

Hipólito Irigoyen

The Great Depression, a financial crisis that shook the world, crushed Argentina's economy. Businesses collapsed, banks were ruined, and people panicked. The army revolted on September 6, 1930, ousting Irigoyen and launching a succession of military governments. It was a very unstable time. Presidents came and went as if through a revolving door. During World War II (1939–1945), the leaders of the army favored Nazi Germany and fascist Italy although Argentina was officially neutral. The nation had strong ties to Germany and many of its officers were trained there. They expected Germany to win the war and deposed President Ramón S. Castillo because they thought he might support the large British community living in Argentina at the time.

Juan Perón

Opponents Arrested

The new regime arrested many labor leaders and liberal politicians. This upset most Argentines. They found a voice in young Juan Perón, an officer who had worked in several

Eva and Juan Perón wave to supporters.

government positions over the years. Perón built a strong following among the workers. He was arrested but then was freed when tens of thousands of his supporters marched to Buenos Aires to demand that he become a candidate for president. Perón was elected and his Labor Party controlled Congress. He ruled for the next nine years, supported by his second wife, María Eva (Evita) Duarte Perón, a movie actress and radio personality. She was said to be the real power in Argentina.

The Peronistas, Perón's followers, shut down opposition publications, restricted other political parties, and wrote their own constitution. As a couple, the Peróns remained popular despite what their followers did. Señora Perón gave a lot a money to the poor, whom she called the "shirtless ones," and snubbed rich people. But she was a vindictive woman and anyone who questioned her motives suffered for it. When Eva Perón died of cancer in 1952 at the age of thirty-three, the entire country mourned.

Perón Flees

Eventually, even Perón lost favor and he fled into exile in Spain in 1955. The Peronistas remained politically active and

Eva Perón

Eva Perón has been the subject of movies, plays, and novels. The most well-known production was a musical about her life, which had the theme song "Don't Cry for Me, Argentina." The musical was made into a movie, *Evita,* with Eva Perón being played by the American singer/actress Madonna. Even after her death, Señora Perón was controversial. Political forces in the country battled for decades over who controlled her corpse. Initially, the military hid her body because they feared it would become a rallying point for the opposition. The body was supposedly stored in an officer's attic until the remains were smuggled out of the country. It was buried under a false name in Italy and remained there for sixteen years. Perón himself recovered the body and returned it to Buenos Aires. Allegedly, he obtained the body by agreeing to support a certain general as president in 1971. The officer was one of the few people who had known where Señora Perón was buried.

tried to disrupt the governments that followed. For a time, there was some stability in Argentina, especially in the regime of Arturo Frondizi. He worked hard to correct the country's economic problems after years of mismanagement. But even that wasn't enough. Can you guess who showed up in elections for president in 1973? Perón again! He was reelected but served only a year before dying in office in 1974. According to the constitution, he was to be succeeded by his vice president, who was his widow. (Perón had married again while in Spain.) The last Señora Perón, María Estela (Isabel) Martínez de Perón took over. She was the first woman to head any nation in the Americas.

However, in 1976, Isabel Perón was deposed by a junta, a group of military officers. A succession of generals then held power. They launched what became known as the Dirty

Juan Perón and wife Isabel watching a giant parade

War to rid the country of leftists and other opponents. They excused their actions by pointing out that former president Pedro Eugenio Aramburu had been kidnapped in 1970 and eventually killed. Many policemen, government officials, and soldiers also had been assassinated. For these reasons, they felt that a firm hand was necessary to prevent lawlessness in Argentina. But thousands of innocent people were imprisoned without trial, tortured, and killed. Today, in Buenos Aires, the Mothers of the Plaza de Mayo march every Thursday demanding to know what happened to their children who were taken away during that terrible era and never seen again.

In 1982, the Argentine military launched a war with the British over the Falkland/Malvinas Islands. The mission was a catastrophe for Argentina and Lieutenant General Leopoldo Galtieri, the ruler at the time, was forced to resign.

In October 1982, lawyer Raúl Alfonsín of the Radical Civic Union was elected president of Argentina. His victory ended the power of the military and the political domination of the Peronistas. In 1989, the country faced an energy crisis, high foreign debt, and severe inflation. (Inflation decreases the value of a country's money.) In mid-1983, the value of the peso was 49,000 pesos=U.S.$1.

Carlos Saúl Menem became president in 1989, taking office five months early so that he could tackle the nation's problems. He reversed five decades of state control over the economy through intensive reform. All businesses owned by the state were put in private hands. Protests erupted when

Raúl Alfonsín

Islas Malvinas or Falklands?

In 1592, English explorer John Davis discovered several windswept hunks of rock 300 miles (480 km) off the east coast of Argentina in the South Atlantic. The islands were suitable primarily for sheep raising. Over the years, the French, the Spanish, and the Argentines also claimed the islands known as the Islas Malvinas in the Spanish language and the Falkland Islands in English. The Argentine government claimed the islands in 1820, but it was not strong enough to keep them. In 1833, the British took the islands back and have held them ever since. Argentine troops invaded East Falkland in 1982 but were driven off by the British. Argentina's only cruiser, the *General Belgrano*, was sunk and more than 1,000 Argentine troops died.

Menem pardoned the military officers involved in the Dirty War, but Menem felt he had to resolve that problem to get the country moving again. So he remained in power. Argentina's quest for economic stability is still going on.

In 1997, Buenos Aires was a stopover for U.S. president Bill Clinton on a widely publicized Latin American tour. Clinton spoke with an audience and answered questions via satellite in a Spanish-language broadcast that was beamed throughout the region. The program was also aired in many cities in the United States. As many as 500 million people heard the program.

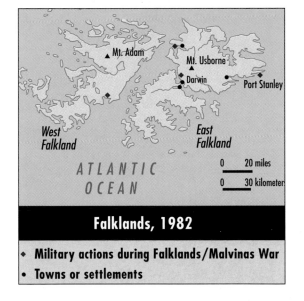

Falklands, 1982

♦ Military actions during Falklands/Malvinas War
• Towns or settlements

Two days later, Clinton and President Menem visited Nahuel Huapí National Park. With a backdrop of the Andes Mountains, the two leaders agreed that their nations should support restrictions on gases that contribute to global warming.

Running the Country

The official name of Argentina is the *República Argentina* (Argentine Republic). Argentina's government functions under the provisions of the 1853 constitution, which was updated in August 1994. Past governments often ignored the basic principles of the constitution to serve their own interests and not those of the people. However, the country remains a federal republic with separate executive, legislative, and judicial branches.

THE EXECUTIVE BRANCH IS HEADED by a president, who is directly elected by the people for a four-year term. Any candidate for president or vice president must meet three official requirements. He or she must be a native-born Argentine, a Roman Catholic, and at least thirty years old. The president is also the head of the military.

President Carlos Saúl Menem of the Justicialist Party (PJ), a Peronista party, was elected on July 8, 1989, and reelected in May 1995. His vice president is Carlos Ruckauf.

President Menem after being sworn in for his second term as president

The president is assisted by a cabinet, whose members are responsible for different jobs. They monitor defense, affairs of state, transportation, education, social services, and arts.

Two-House Legislature

According to the constitution, the legislature, called the *Congreso Nacional* (Argentine National Congress), consists of two houses—the Senate and the Chamber of Deputies. The Senate consists of two members from each of Argentina's

Opposite: **Argentine National Congress**

PACIFIC OCEAN

CHILE · JUJUY · PARAGUAY

SALTA · FORMOSA

TUCUMÁN · CHACO

CATAMARCA · SANTIAGO DEL ESTERO · MISIONES

CORRIENTES

LA RIOJA · SANTA FE · BRAZIL

SAN JUAN · CÓRDOBA · ENTRE RÍOS

MENDOZA · SAN LUIS · URUGUAY

ARGENTINA · Buenos Aires

LA PAMPA · BUENOS AIRES

NEUQUÉN

RÍO NEGRO

CHUBUT

ATLANTIC OCEAN

SANTA CRUZ

0 — 200 miles
0 — 300 kilometers

Provinces

Argentina's Provinces

Argentina's provinces are Buenos Aires, Catamarca, Chaco, Chubut, Córdoba, Corrientes, Entre Ríos, Formosa, Jujuy, La Pampa, La Rioja, Mendoza, Misiones, Neuquén, Río Negro, Salta, San Juan, San Luis, Santa Cruz, Santa Fe, Santiago del Estero and Tucumán. There is also one national territory consisting of Tierra del Fuego, the Antarctic and the South Atlantic islands; plus one federal district of Buenos Aires, the capital city. Each is headed by a governor, elected by voters.

provinces. Senators are elected by their local legislatures for nine-year terms. Members of the Chamber of Deputies are elected by voters and must be at least twenty-five years old. A deputy's term runs for four years.

Getting Out the Vote

In Argentina, unlike many other countries, voting is compulsory for all citizens between the ages of eighteen and seventy. However, a voter may be excused if he or she is in the military or the clergy, or lives too far from a polling place (a place where people go to vote). A person who is sick is also excused from voting. Some people, such as criminals, are deprived of the right to vote.

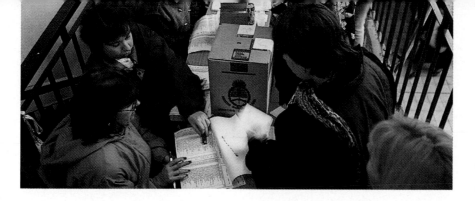

Voting is compulsory in Argentina.

Parties and Patriots

Argentina has many political parties. Almost everyone in the country takes a keen interest in government affairs—or at least has strong opinions on the issues, the personalities, and how the country is run. People love talking about politics in cafés, on street corners, at union halls, and between soccer matches on Sunday afternoons.

The modern political party system originated in Argentina in the late 1890s when the Radical Party was founded. For the next five decades, the country's political life was a verbal clash between the middle-class Radicals and the rich landowners and industrialists with their close ties to Europe. This tradition was shaken up in the 1940s, with the emergence of the Peronistas. They favored President Juan Perón, sought social reform, supported unions, and wanted an economy that was free from foreign domination. Their slogan was "labor is the government and the government is labor."

In Argentina, a strong individual can often take over a political party for his own purposes. A leader who speaks well, rouses the crowds, and brings in money for his political organization is usually sure to be elected. Such a person, called a *caudillo* (political strongman), sometimes ruled by force and terror in the nineteenth-century days of

Buenos Aires: Did You Know This?

Buenos Aires is a cosmopolitan, exciting city that never seems to sleep. Its mix of nationalities gives Buenos Aires a European style, with traditions of the Old World combined with the energy of the Americas. By 1995, more than 12 million people lived in the metropolitan area, up from only 3.5 million in 1956. Many rural people have moved to Buenos Aires in search of jobs. Buenos Aires has been a port since 1580, so its citizens are called *porteños*. The city's name, given by the sailors who founded it, means "Fair Winds" in Spanish.

Plaza de Mayo (below) is Buenos Aires' oldest square, dating back to 1580 when it was called *Plaza Mayor*

(Principal Square). Adjacent to the plaza is the Casa Rosada, the seat of the executive branch of government; the Cabildo, the colonial town hall; and the Metropolitan Cathedral.

Ezeiza International Airport, forty-five minutes from downtown Buenos Aires, serves flights from around the world. Taxis, *colectivos* (buses), and the *subte* (subway) link the airport to the downtown business district. The glazed tiles in the subway stations were handmade in Spain.

Avenida 9 de Julio (above), the world's widest street, was made 425 feet wide (130 m) by knocking down all the buildings that were once in its center. The *Obelisco* (obelisk) at the Plaza de la República on the avenue commemorates the city's 400th anniversary.

The average daily temperature is 74°F (23.3°C) in January and 50°F (7°C) in July.

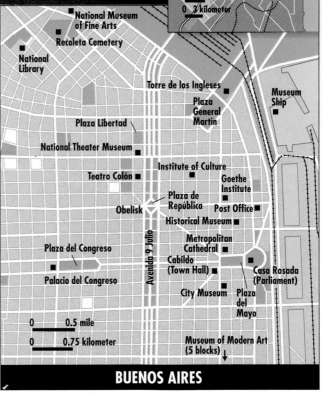

Rio de la Plata

Area of Detail

Buenos Aires

0   2 miles
0   3 kilometer

National Museum of Fine Arts
Recoleta Cemetery
National Library
Torre de los Ingleses
Museum Ship
Plaza General Martin
Plaza Libertad
National Theater Museum
Institute of Culture
Teatro Colón
Goethe Institute
Plaza de República
Obelisk
Post Office
Historical Museum
Metropolitan Cathedral
Plaza del Congreso
Cabildo (Town Hall)
Casa Rosada (Parliament)
Palacio del Congreso
Avenida 9 de Julio
City Museum
Plaza del Mayo

0   0.5 mile
0   0.75 kilometer

Museum of Modern Art (5 blocks) ↓

BUENOS AIRES

Carlos Saúl Menem

Argentina's president is Carlos Saúl Menem, a lawyer and career politician. He was governor of La Rioja province before his election to the presidency in 1989. A constitutional change allowed him to run again and he was reelected in 1995. Menem was a follower of Juan Perón. He received a law degree from the University of Córdoba in 1955 and has held numerous public and political offices since the 1960s. He spent five years in prison and internal exile after a 1976 military coup ousted President Isabel Perón.

Menem was born on July 2, 1930, in Argentina, the son of Sunni Muslim immigrants from Syria. Menem has since converted to Catholicism. He and his wife have a son and a daughter.

He has advocated a free-market system in Argentina, contrary to the traditional view of his Justicialist Party. In the past, his party favored central government control over all aspects of production and was hostile to the United States. But Menem now advocates close business and cultural ties with Argentina's North American neighbor.

Presidents Rosas and Urquiza. Modern caudillos have been more subtle, counting on their ability to get votes. And behind this rocky surface of Argentine politics, the support of the armed forces has been necessary to the success of most national leaders.

The military consists of the army, navy, *gendarmerie* (national police), and coast guard. About 153,000 persons serve in the armed forces, including about 100,000 army personnel. The active troop strength is 70,000. The military feels it must protect the country not only from outside aggression but also from internal revolt. So the military thinks it has every right to interfere in politics.

From 1860 to 1916, the military was loyal to Argentina's conservative governments. When it deposed the Radical Party in 1930, that set the stage for later intervention. Between 1930 and 1989, there were six military coups and

Opposite, bottom: **Armed force was necessary to quell the rioting by Peronistas during the 1960s.**

Soldiers guarding the Casa Rosada after a military junta took control of the government from Isabel Perón

Argentina's National Flag

The Argentine national flag consists of three equal horizontal bands. Two light-blue bands are separated by a white band. Centered in the white band is a radiant yellow sun with a human face known as the Sun of May. On the country's coat of arms, adopted in 1813, a cap symbolizes liberty and hands clasp each other to represent brotherhood and unity.

A political rally during Carlos Menem's campaign for the presidency

almost twenty years of outright military rule. From 1952 until 1989, no elected president was able to serve his term without being forced from office. More than half of Argentina's rulers have been generals or members of a junta, a coalition of officers. The military's budget is about $4.7 billion a year.

In addition to President Carlos Saúl Menem's party, other political organizations include the Radical Civic Union, a moderate, left-of-center party; the Union of the Democratic Center, a conservative group; the Dignity and Independence Political Party, a right-wing party; the Grand Front, a center-left mix of several small parties; and the Front for a Country in Solidarity, another coalition of four political groups. The provinces have a number of political parties.

Rallies Held

During elections, all these parties hold massive rallies, parades, and strategy meetings. Thousands turn out to support their favorite candidates, waving banners and wearing special uniforms and caps with fluttering ribbons pinned to their jackets. Bands play, speeches are given in town

Argentine National Anthem

Spanish	English Translation
¡Oid mortales! el grito sagrado:	Mortals! Hear the sacred cry;
¡Libertad, Libertad, Libertad!	Freedom! Freedom! Freedom!
Oid el ruido de rotas cadenas:	Hear the noise of broken chains.
Ved in trono a la noble Igualdad.	See noble Equality enthroned.
¡Ya su trono dignísimo abrieron	The United Provinces of the South
Las provincias unidas del Sud!	Have now displayed their worthy throne.
Y los libres del mundo responden:	And the free peoples of the world reply:
¡Al Gran Pueblo Argentino Salud!	We salute the great people of Argentina!
(repeat)	(repeat)
Y los libres del mundo responden:	And the free peoples of the world reply:
¡Al Gran Pueblo Argentino Salud!	We salute the great people of Argentina!
(repeat previous two lines)	(repeat previous two lines)
CHORUS	**CHORUS**
Sean eternos los laureles	May the laurels be eternal
Que supimos conseguir.	That we knew how to win.
Coronados de gloria vivamos	Let us live crowned with glory,
O juiremos con gloria morir.	Or swear to die gloriously.
(repeat three times)	(repeat three times)

Lyrics by: Vincente López y Planes, 1813
Music by: Blas Parera, 1813

squares, and advertisements blare out on TV and radio. Everyone sings the national anthem, "*¡Oid mortales! el grito sagrado: ¡Libertad!*" ("Hear mortals, the sacred cry of Liberty!").

Courts, Consortiums, and Consulates

The Argentine judiciary consists of a Supreme Court, whose nine members are appointed for life by the president. The

State House of Justice in Buenos Aires

Senate gives final approval on all legislation. Federal courts cover cases that involve the constitution and national treaties. Lower courts handle routine civil and criminal cases, from business law to traffic offenses. The legal system is a mixture of U.S. and western European methods.

Argentina takes its responsibilities as a nation seriously. As a member of the United Nations and the World Bank, it has signed numerous agreements with other nations. For regional matters in South America and the Caribbean, Argentina belongs to an association, or consortium, called the Organization of American States. Argentine embassies operate in the capitals of many nations, as well as in Washington, D.C. Consulate offices are established in many U.S. cities. The consulates help with business matters, arrange passports, and host Argentine officials on official state visits.

Rich in Resources

If any country in South America has economic potential, it is Argentina. It is rich in natural resources. Its people are energetic, brimming with creativity. Such a combination can only be good for Argentina.

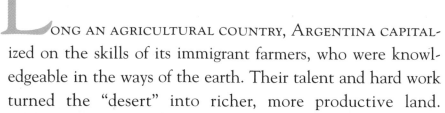

ONG AN AGRICULTURAL COUNTRY, ARGENTINA CAPITAL-
ized on the skills of its immigrant farmers, who were knowl-
edgeable in the ways of the earth. Their talent and hard work
turned the "desert" into richer, more productive land.

Argentine beef is exported around the world.

Argentina has long been the granary
of the world. Corn, wheat, soybeans,
and sorghum are the major cash crops,
along with grapes, sugarcane, tobacco,
cotton, and tea. Animal products are
also important. There are 40,000
dairies in Argentina to process milk
and excellent cheese. Some of the
hamburger eaten in the United States
comes from Argentine beef. Leather
products are also exported. Sheep
farmers export up to 202,200 tons of
wool each year.

Ocean Harvest

With access to the Atlantic Ocean,
many Argentines work in the fishing
industry. About 900,000 tons of fish
and seafood are processed annually—
for Argentines as well as for export.
Langostino, a large shellfish in the
shrimp family, is an important product. The freshwater pejerrey, a type of
kingfish, is also valuable.

An Argentine fisher

Argentine manufacturers produce refrigerators, washing machines, paper and wood pulp, steel tubes, yarn, ships, synthetic rubber, textiles, beer, cement, drugs, cereals, chemical products, cars, and trucks. Brazil is one of Argentina's major trading partners. In 1997, the United States also started importing free-range Argentine beef for the first time in sixty-seven years. A recall of American beef tainted with E. coli bacteria meant there was a shortage that needed to be filled.

Argentina is considered the most open, least protectionist country in the world. Some nations like to limit the amount of goods allowed across their borders. These countries would rather sell overseas than have to import items. But Argentina's healthy businesses also export many goods and products, so the country has a good balance of trade.

The United States and Canada import 15 percent of Argentina's exports, with Europe importing up to 30 percent of its exports each year. Foreign investors are welcome in Argentina and are treated equally

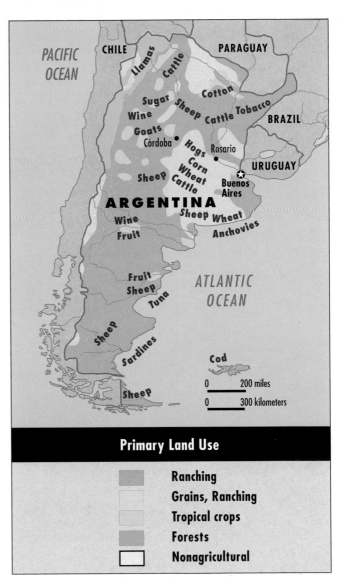

Primary Land Use

- Ranching
- Grains, Ranching
- Tropical crops
- Forests
- Nonagricultural

A Thriving Wine Industry

Argentina produces more than 4 million gallons (15 million l) of wine annually, of which 20 percent are fine wines. The country is one of the five largest wine-producing nations in the world, with more than 490,000 acres (198,000 ha) of vineyards. The country's wide variety of wines include chardonnay, sauvignon, torrontes, and malbec.

Argentina's good soil, favorable weather, modern technology, and skilled workers make its wine industry a major income producer.

Wine making began here in the mid-1500s when the Spanish planted the first vineyards at Santiago del Estero. For generations, wine was produced mainly for Argentines, but intensive international promotional campaigns have made wine exports important. Wine shipments out of Argentina increased 900 percent in 1995. Exports of red wine to the United States increased nearly 140 percent in the first four months of 1995, compared to the same period in 1994.

Autos manufactured for export to Brazil

under the law. Foreigners do not have to pay extra taxes or other fees. Companies from Europe, Asia, and North America are active investors in Argentina.

Under the Table

There is sometimes a dark side of business in Argentina. Some investors complain that government officials expect to receive bribes from foreign investors who want to

A black-market street vendor in Córdoba

set up business in Argentina. There is also a strong black market, where goods are sold under the table to avoid paying taxes. It is estimated that as many as 38 percent of the workers in the city of Córdoba get jobs through the black market. In addition,

What Argentina Grows, Makes, and Mines

Agriculture (1995)

Sugarcane	16.5 million metric tons
Soybeans	12.0 million metric tons
Corn	11.3 million metric tons

Manufacturing (1994)

Cement	6.3 million metric tons
Wheat flour	3.3 million metric tons
Vegetable oil	3.0 million metric tons

Mining (1993)

Petroleum products	22.1 million metric tons
Coal	167,000 metric tons
Crude petroleum	216.8 million barrels

Argentine Currency

In 1992, the new peso replaced the old as the basic unit of Argentine money. There are one hundred centavos in a peso. There are also coins in denominations of one, two, and five pesos, and one, five, ten, twenty-five, and fifty centavos. Portraits of Argentine political leaders are on the currency, which comes in denominations of two, five, ten, twenty, fifty, and one hundred pesos. In 1998, the exchange rate was Arg$1.00=U.S.$1.00.

there is a growing problem with drugs being shipped through Argentina to Europe and the United States.

Argentina wants to be as independent as possible. Yet it realizes it must work closely with other nations in these days of a global economy. Argentina is a member of the Association for Latin American Integration and the Latin American Economic System. These international groups keep lines of communication open between governments and businesses, promoting a free flow of trade. Argentina has set up a free trade zone with Brazil, Paraguay, and Uruguay allowing goods to flow between these countries without taxes.

Getting Around

Argentina's merchant marine fleet carries about 50 percent of the goods produced in Argentina. The service is important to a country that has always depended on the sea for its contact with the outside world. Ocean travel is handled by the 1,413 ships in the State Merchant Fleet. Of these, 176 vessels are oil tankers, but there are also bulk cargo, railcar, and refrigerated cargo carriers. Domestic travel on the nation's 6,820 miles (11,000 km) of navigable rivers is supervised by the Flota Fluvial del Estado Argentina, a government agency. Private shipping lines also operate in Argentina.

The shipping fleet is supported by transportation from the interior to the ports. Roads radiate out from Buenos Aires to the provinces, a heritage from the colonial days. The total distance covered by main roads in Argentina is 1.3 million miles (2.1 million km). Of these, 38,092 miles (61,440 km) are paved. And the nation has 23,504 miles (37,910 km) of railroads. English investors helped Argentina build its extensive rail system. The trains carry almost 500 million passengers annually, as well as freight.

Argentina is such a long country that it needs an extensive, well-kept transportation network. Many challenges face road builders, especially in the Andes. One engineering marvel is the Christ Redeemer Tunnel that links Argentina's Highway 7 with Chile's Highway 60. The tunnel is 10,106 feet

Huge cranes facilitate the loading of exports on ocean vessels.

(3,080 m) long, with thousands of feet of approach roads. The Puerto Unzue-Fray Bentos Bridge between Argentina and Uruguay is another amazing structure at 7,756 feet (2,364 m) long.

Countries Served

Aerolinas Argentinas, the national airline, has a fleet of modern planes that serve Australia, North and South America, and Europe. Argentina has 1,253 airports of all sizes. The Ezeiza International Airport is 19 miles (30 km) from downtown Buenos Aires. Domestic flights use the Aeroparque City of Buenos Aires, on the banks of the Río de la Plata. It also connects fliers to Montevideo and other cities in Uruguay and to Brazil.

Cars waiting to pass through the Christ Redeemer Tunnel

Petroleum Producer

Argentina is now taking full advantage of its oil and gas reserves and is increasing its industrial output, especially in chemical manufacturing. There are new dams, factories, roads, and airports to accommodate growing business. A state-operated facility, the Yacimentos Petroliferos Fiscales helps private corporations find new oil wells. These wells meet more than 90 percent of the oil needs in Argentina. Thousands of miles of pipeline connect the oil fields with processing plants.

Gas, Coal, and Water Power

The country has other riches—enough natural gas to last at least another 100 years, according to government reports, and important coal deposits in the south. More than 727,000 tons of coal are mined annually by Hierro Patagonico, the country's major mining company. Argentina also has extensive deposits of gold, iron ore, lead, limestone, manganese, mica, silver, tin, tungsten, and zinc.

Power plants are necessary to run Argentine industry, so the swiftest rivers are harnessed by massive dams. The rushing water powers giant turbines that produce electrical energy. Often, the river flows along a national border so Argentina and its neighbor cooperate in building a power plant. One such project benefited both Argentina and Uruguay.

A fuel depot in Ushuaia

A massive hydroelectric dam on the Paraguay-Argentine border

Nuclear-Waste Disposal

Disposal of radioactive wastes has been an ongoing problem in Argentina. In 1980, the government awarded funds to Cuyo University in San Juan province for the study of potential sites for medium to high-level nuclear-waste disposal. The chosen area was in Sierra del Medio, near Gastre, about 868 miles (1,400 km) south of Buenos Aires. Work started in 1986, with construction due to be complete by 2002. In 1996, a large demonstration by angry citizens protested a government plan to import nuclear waste from France and bury it at Gastre.

Because of public protests, that project was delayed until 2030. The cost of the disposal site, including roads leading to the dump, was expected to reach $3 billion.

Three provinces—Neuquén, Río Negro, and Tierra del Fuego—have banned the storage or transfer of radioactive material through their territory.

Nuclear Power

Argentina was the first South American country to have a nuclear power station. The plant, built in 1974 at Atucha, 62 miles (100 km) north of Buenos Aires, handles 7 percent of the nation's power needs. The facility also serves as a training site for technicians from other South American countries. The Institute Balseiro, in San Carlos de Bariloche in the southern Andes, also trains nuclear workers. Several other nuclear plants were built in the 1980s and another six started in the 1990s are due to be completed by 2000. Argentina can even mine its own uranium as fuel. In 1995, Argentina announced that private investors, rather than the government, would be operating the new nuclear power plants. A new corporation called Nucleoéléctrica Argentina was formed for this purpose, but the effort failed. Attempts continued at the end of the 1990s to revitalize the private ownership of the nuclear power industry.

Union Power

While Argentina has a highly capable, efficient workforce of more than 10 million, 16 percent of the population is unemployed. It is hoped that more foreign investment in industry and research will help alleviate that problem.

Unions have always been strong in Argentina, largely because of the European heritage of most Argentines. Labor activists who immigrated to the country over the past generations brought their ideals of fair representation and worker-management cooperation with them. Depending on which government was in power, the unions either have held a position of responsibility or have been persecuted. President Juan Perón based much of his support on unions and actively courted their money, votes, and voices. Several Peronista unions are still hard at work years after his death. The General Confederation of Labor is the largest of these.

Countering the union movement is the Argentine Industrial Union (a manufacturers' association). In the countryside, the Argentine Rural Society represents the large landowners, while several small agricultural unions speak for farmworkers.

Headquarters for the Social Security Institute

Social Security and Benefits

Argentina has a strong social security system. Businesses have a pension requirement ensuring that people receive an income after they retire. And there are subsidies for older citizens who were unable to contribute to pension funds. In Argentina, the government takes care of disability payments, too. This helps injured workers who can't return to their jobs. Sickness, hospitalization, and vacation allowances are worked out between industry and the country's strong unions. Argentina is a solidly middle-class country, with living standards similar to those in Europe.

Many Faces of Argentina

The first Argentines were Native Americans whose early ancestors crossed the frozen Bering Sea from Asia to North America in the ancient past. After fanning out across North America, these early people eventually made their way south. The first groups arrived at the southernmost tip of South America by 9000 B.C. Archaeologists have found cave dwellings near the Strait of Magellan dating back as far as that, and other such prehistoric homes are scattered throughout southern Argentina. The best known are at Las Cueva de las Manos, outside the village of Perito Moreno.

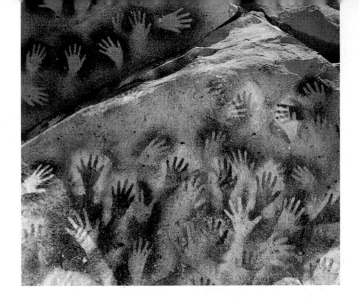

THE WALLS THERE ARE DECORATED with hunting and harvesting scenes. However, the Native American population was small in the Argentine region. Only about 300,000 Native Americans lived throughout this vast area. The largest group belonged to the Guaraní people, who were principally farmers, in what is now northeastern Argentina. Around A.D. 1480, Inca armies from Peru invaded and incorporated the area into their empire. Some of their walled towns had as many as 3,000 residents.

Handprints made by humans more than 7,000 years ago

Opposite: **An assistant at a polo match**

A Guaraní Indian displays handmade crafts.

Formidable Warriors

Nomadic Native Americans lived on the Pampa and in the far south. Their lifestyle remained relatively unchanged for at least 6,000 years, until the Spanish brought horses. The Native Americans soon became formidable warriors and were not totally defeated until the early 1900s. Other Native Americans lived in the Andes Mountains and in the rain forests.

A mestizo girl

Most died of diseases brought by the Europeans or were killed in the long wars that followed the Spanish invasion in 1516. Today, only 50,000—or about 3 percent of Argentines—are Native Americans. This is a far cry from the number who lived in Argentina in the 1500s.

Today, Argentina is primarily European. Eighty-five percent of the people are white and the remaining 15 percent are mixed-race, Native American, or other nonwhite groups. Many of the early settlers were mestizo—people of mixed European and Indian heritage. This mixture of heritages is most easily seen in the faces of the gauchos, the hard-riding cowboys of the Pampa. Their brown skin and high cheekbones are signs of their Native American ancestry.

Rich colonists were able to bring wives from Spain. Their upper-class children were called Creoles, meaning persons born in Argentina to parents of Spanish descent. Few Argentines are of African descent because slavery never played a major role in the country's agricultural system. Slavery, in fact, was abolished in 1813.

Revolutionary Leaders

Mulattoes are Argentines whose parents are a mix of white and black or Native American or any other combination. Though they were often looked down upon, the mulattoes were leaders in Argentina's struggle for independence. They felt they had nothing to lose by fighting for freedom. Many of these experienced soldiers went on to serve other South American countries in their wars for independence.

Early European immigrants arriving in Buenos Aires

By the time Argentina became independent in 1816, most of its population had been born in South America. That situation changed in the mid-1800s when a wave of newcomers arrived in Argentina. Swiss and Germans settled around Buenos Aires and Santa Fe. Other Europeans settled on remote farms and in distant villages where they could keep up their own traditions. Later on, hundreds of thousands of other European settlers appeared on Argentina's doorstep. Many were Italians and Spaniards who helped open the vast Pampa to farming and ranching. A worldwide demand for Argentine beef, tallow, hides, wool, and mutton meant that more workers were needed.

Immigrant Workers

Many immigrants had to become tenant farmers because so much of the land belonged to wealthy families. Tenant farmers rent the land where they raise their crops. It was hard for a poor person to buy land, so most newcomers settled in the cities and worked in mills, packinghouses, and granaries. They lived in neighborhoods made up entirely of their ethnic group. They had their own clubs, newspapers, and sports teams. The English

The Swallows

Temporary workers from Europe who came to Argentina in the early 1900s were called the Swallows because they came and went across the Atlantic. In the spring, they helped with the planting and in the autumn they returned for the harvest. Because the seasons were just the opposite of those in their homeland, they could work on farms year-round.

Immigrants moving to the Argentine interior to work as farmers

Newly arrived Jewish immigrants

loved polo. The Italians played bocce ball, a form of lawn bowling. This mixture of traditions, foods, and lifestyles gave Argentina its fascinating blend of cultures.

The expansion of the nation's rail network, developed by English and Scottish engineers, helped other immigrants find homes throughout Argentina. By the time World War I (1914–1918) broke out, 30 percent of the population was foreign-born, but they were readily assimilated into the Argentine culture. Following World War II (1939–1945), another—more desperate—group flooded into Argentina: war refugees. Most were German and Jewish professionals and similar highly skilled individuals who settled primarily in Misiones and put another interesting stamp on the face of Argentina. In the 1980s, newcomers came from war-torn Southeast Asia. Because the constitution of 1853 gives equal rights to all citizens, regardless of their heritage, Argentina welcomed everyone.

This liberal immigration policy has always been important to the country's growth and spirit. Political scientist Juan Bautista Alberdi, "the Father of the Argentine Constitution," believed that to govern was to populate. He invited many people to live in his country and to become hard-working, productive citizens. He knew that openness would make Argentina a leader in South America. Alberdi's dream was successful. By 1900, only two years' residency was required to become an Argentine citizen. Resident foreigners were glad they did not have to serve in the military. Children of these newcomers moved into highly skilled jobs in business, industry, education, science, and the arts. Looking at a Buenos Aires phone book tells the tale of many nationalities.

Languages of Argentina

The official language of Argentina is Spanish, although language experts have identified twenty-six individual Native American tongues. The Argentines refer to their Spanish form of speaking as Castellano. They talk very fast, so it is often hard to understand them unless the listener is an Argentine, too. The original Spanish language is flavored with a special blend of accents and expressions. Every part of the country has its own dialect and pronunciation, so it easy for Argentines to identify a stranger's home province.

Students are often heard speaking Spanish mixed with Italian words.

Pronunciation Key

One of the more obvious differences between Spanish and Castellano is the pronunciation of the "ll," as in "llama." In Spanish, "ll" is pronounced *ya* as in "yama." But in Castellano, "ll" has a *z* and *sh* sound, becoming "zhama."

Vowels in Castellano are pronounced as in English or Spanish:

"a" is pronounced *ah* as in "dart"

"e" is pronounced *ay* as in "they"

"i" is pronounced *ee* as in "sleep"

"o" is pronounced *oh* as in "owe"

"u" is pronounced *oo* as in "spoon."

There are some differences in consonants:

"ñ" as in "niño" is pronounced *ny* as in "canyon"

"j" as in "jabón" is pronounced *h* as in "habitat"

"c" before "e" or "i" is pronounced *s* as in "sentry."

Argentine Spanish is also heavily influenced by Italian. This is not surprising because there are more Argentines of Italian descent than of Spanish ancestry. On the streets and in the cafés, young people often use the Italian greeting *buongiorno* rather than the Spanish *buenos días*. When saying good-bye, they often casually toss out "chau" (pronounced "chow"), which is the Spanish spelling of the Italian *ciao*.

Pronouns and Pronunciation

In South America, personal pronouns such as "I," "you," "he," "she," "we," and "they" are seldom used because they are incorporated into the verbs. Friends in Argentina use the familiar word *che* for "you." The second person *tú* became *vos*, a

Where Is the Bathroom?

The Argentine word for "toilet" is *servicio* or baño. The men's room is marked for *hombres* or *caballeros*. The women's room is for *senoras* or *damas*. If someone asks, "¿Dónde está el baño para caballeros?," they are asking the way to the men's room. Sometimes, in polite Argentine society, the bathrooms are called the *excusado*. This literally means "the excused."

shortening of the word *vosotros*, the plural form of *tú* used in Spain. Some words are different in both Spanish and Castellano. "Money" is *dinero* in the original Spanish, but is *yira* in Argentina. In Spanish, the fruit "avocado" is *aguacate*, but in Argentina, it is called *palta*.

It is also important to put the emphasis on the correct syllable or a word may take on an entirely different meaning. For example, Argentine youngsters say *papá*, which means "father." The stress is on the final "a,"—pa-PA. If the first "a" is stressed, the word becomes *papa*, which means "potato."

Native American Languages

Several of Argentina's native languages are also spoken in Bolivia, Peru, and Chile. As various Indian populations moved through these areas over the centuries, they left their language behind. This linguistic impact is still heard. For instance, a Spanish speaker would have a hard time understanding many of the Bolivian sugar-mill hands who now

work in Argentina. These workers speak a rare language called Aymara. Yet, more than 2 million Argentines speak Aymara as their first language.

Fifteen thousand Argentines speak Chiriguano and 11,000 speak Chiripá. Several other languages are almost extinct. In the early 1990s, social scientists could identify only five families in east-central Chaco province who still spoke Vilela. The Vilela culture was gradually being absorbed into other native groups and their language is expected to disappear by 2000.

In Buenos Aires, some people speak a mishmash of immigrant languages based on Castellano. This mishmash is a fast-paced slang called *Lunfardo*, which allows people from diverse cultural backgrounds and tongues to understand each other. Many Argentines also speak fluent English, German, Italian, French, and other languages. There are some villages where the residents speak mostly Welsh because their grandparents came from Wales as shepherds.

Some experts even count hand signing as one of the country's designated languages. Argentine schools for the hearing-impaired were started in 1885 and deaf children have used sign language for decades.

Migrant Workers and City People

In addition to its widely diversified population, Argentina hires inexpensive foreign workers to help it grow and remain economically strong. This is especially true in farming. Argentina's farms have fewer tractors and specialized farm equipment than those in the United States and Canada,

Common Spanish Phrases Used in Argentina	
Good morning	Buenos días
Good afternoon	Buenas tardes
Good night	Buenas noches
See you again	Hasta la vista
How are you?	¿Cómo está usted?
Fine, thanks. And you?	¿Bien, gracias. Y usted?
Merry Christmas	Feliz Navidad
I'm sorry	Lo siento
Please speak more slowly.	Habla más despacio, por favor.
What time is it?	¿Qué hora es?

Opposite: **A wide mix of languages can be heard on Buenos Aires' streets.**

Many foreign workers have made their homes in Argentina. This family is from Bolivia.

so thousands of workers are needed to help plant and harvest. Between December and March, Paraguayans help with the maté harvest in Misiones. Maté is a plant used to make a popular tea. Workers from Chile and Bolivia help pick grapes from April to July in Mendoza and Cuyo. Workers from other South American countries help with the cotton, tobacco, and sugarcane harvests in northern Argentina. While most workers go home in the off-season, a growing number enjoy life in Argentina and prefer to stay. As a result, more Paraguayans live in Buenos Aires than in Asunción, the capital city of Paraguay. In northwest Argentina, Bolivians have found a welcome, and a steady number of Chileans are moving to Patagonia. Like their precedessors, these latest arrivals find that Argentina has a lot to offer.

Argentina is now primarily an urban nation, with more than 70 percent of its 34,995,000 citizens living in cities or towns. One-third of the nation's population—12 million residents—live in bustling Buenos Aires, the capital, and its suburbs. By the early 1980s, seventeen other cities had populations greater than 100,000. The remaining 30 percent of Argentina's people work on farms or live in small villages on the Pampa, in the mountain valleys, and along the coasts. By 2010, the population is expected to be 40,193,000, and by 2025, the population is projected to total 45,505,000.

Population of Major Cities (1996 est.)	
Buenos Aires	2,960,976
(Greater Buenos Aires)	12,582,321
Córdoba	1,208,713
Rosario	1,078,374
La Plata	542,567

A Young Population

With the wave of new arrivals between 1900 and 1917, most of the Argentine people were under twenty-five years old. Because the nation was primarily rural at that time, these young people were needed to work in the fields. But in recent years, with the growth of the cities, the thirty-to-fifty age group has become predominant.

Yet Argentina remains a relatively young country, with about 30 percent of the population under fifteen years old. In a 1996 census, there were 4.9 million boys and 4.7 million girls under fourteen years old. Argentina has a comfortable lifestyle as well as fine medical services and plenty of food. As a result, most Argentine men live to be sixty-nine or seventy and most women live to be seventy-five or older.

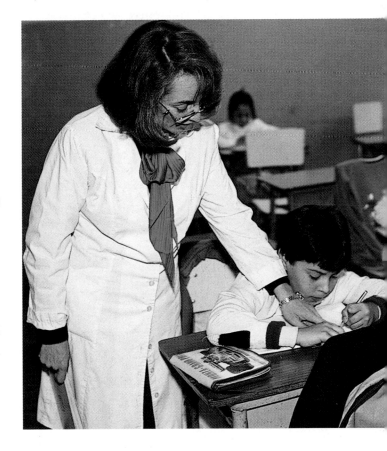

Both students and teachers in Argentina typically wear white coats.

Education and Equal Rights

Almost everyone in Argentina can read and write, even in the remote parts of the country. Education has been accepted by the government as an important responsibility. President Domingo Faustina Sarmiento, who ruled Argentina from 1868 to 1874, was a leader in promoting high standards of education.

Every child must attend seven years of primary school, which is free. Today, more than 5 million youngsters between the ages of six and fourteen attend classes. Schools are run by the provinces; the city of Buenos Aires is responsible for its own school administration. Tuition is charged in private schools throughout the country.

In many public schools, the students wear uniforms. They study reading, math, science, history, and art.

High school is also free at state schools. There are two divisions—basic and higher. In the basic division, students learn the fundamentals of more difficult subjects. In their last two years, they specialize in several areas, from farming to the arts.

Specialty Schools

About 500,000 young people attend universities and technical schools, and many adults go to evening classes. There are specialty schools for teachers, for sports instructors, and for the arts and other fields. Argentina has many schools of higher learning, including twenty-five national, one provincial, and thirty-three private universities. Many students go on to earn higher degrees after they graduate from a university.

Women have equal rights in Argentina. They make up about 50 percent of the population. Since the 1940s, Argentine women have been a major part of the workforce. Professional women include lawyers, doctors, and others. They are active politically too, as we have seen in the governmental roles of Juan Perón's wives, Eva and Isabel.

Argentine Universities

The first university in Argentina was established at Córdoba in 1613. Other national universities were founded in Buenos Aires in 1821, San Miguel de Tucumán in 1914, Santa Fe in 1919, Mendoza in 1939, Bahía Blanca in 1956, Corrientes in 1957, and Santa Rosa in 1959.

The Spiritual Side of Life

The religion of Argentina is Roman Catholicism. The Spanish were devout Catholics when they arrived in the 1500s, so religion was a major factor in the colonial administration. The Spanish felt it was important to build churches as well as forts and villages. The bishops and cardinals who made up the Catholic hierarchy became very powerful and often had huge estates of their own. The clergy subtly influenced government policy because the politicians did not want to offend them.

R ELIGIOUS BELIEFS WERE DEEPLY ingrained in the spirit of the Argentines. They were a prayerful people. During the fight for independence, the battle flag of General José de San Martín carried the name and image of Buenos Aires' patron saint, Martin of Tours. The Hungarian saint lived and died in France, his adopted country, and never visited Argentina. He was canonized (made a saint) for his work with the poor and downtrodden.

San Isidro Cathedral in the Buenos Aires suburbs

Saints and Sinners

Martin almost failed to qualify as Buenos Aires' patron saint. The city's founders wanted Buenos Aires to have a patron but there were many excellent, equally holy candidates. Some residents leaned toward a Spanish saint, since the city was settled by Spaniards. In the end, they put the names of their candidates on slips of paper and drew the winner out of a hat. According to the legend, every name pulled was that of Martin of Tours. So the Argentines agreed that he should be the one.

Opposite: **The interior of a cathedral in Salta**

The early missionaries welcomed the opportunity to work with the Native American population. These first missionaries were Franciscans and Dominicans, followed by the Jesuits. Early in the 1600s, the Spanish built towns called *reducciones* for the Native Americans. It was believed that gathering the Indians in centralized areas would make them easier to "civilize" and to convert to Christianity. In 1609, the Spanish king gave the Jesuits permission to make a major effort to convert the Guaraní tribe. The Jesuits built missions at Nuestra Senora de Loreto and other locations in the Misiones province. The Indians were taught crafts, farming skills, and trades.

A copperplate engraving of Jesuit missionaries in Argentina

Missions Attacked

Many settlers, however, looked down on the Indians and drove them from their homes. Then in 1630, the missions themselves were attacked by slave hunters from Brazil. Thousands of Indians died and thousands more tried to escape to safety beyond the Guairá Falls on the Río Paraná. Most were captured or killed. The Jesuits' objections to the brutal treatment of the people under their care were ignored by the government. The Spanish government wanted the mission property for the growing European population. They could make money from farming, mining, and logging in the areas occupied by the Native Americans. The Jesuits were replaced by Franciscans and forced to leave South America in 1728. Settlers then moved onto the mission lands and destroyed the buildings. Most of the Indians went back into the rain forests. Their traditional shamans (priests) urged them to return to the old ways. The ruins of those Jesuit missions are major tourist attractions today.

In the 1880s, abuse of Church influence resulted in a wave of public outrages. Politicians and people on the street made fun of priests, ministers, and rabbis. No religious denomination was spared. However, this attitude did not last long and all was forgotten in a few years.

Freedom to Worship

New arrivals to Argentina are accepted more readily if they are Catholic, although people of all faiths were generally welcome. Affirming this open attitude, Article Fourteen of the

A synagogue in Buenos Aires

country's constitution of 1853 guarantees freedom of religion. Yet the country is still primarily Roman Catholic, though most people attend church services only on holidays. Today, about 2.5 percent of the Argentines are Protestant, with a growing number of "born-again Christians." Evangelists such as Carlos Annacondia conduct crusades where people make a public commitment to change their ways. In La Plata, near Buenos Aires, a maximum-security prison for 4,000 inmates has a "Christian floor," where inmates can hold prayer meetings and avoid the rougher prisoners.

Two percent of Argentines, or approximately 700,000 people, are Jewish. The Jewish Colonization Association helped Jewish settlers become established in Argentina mostly in the 1880s. Many settled in Entre Ríos province and others spread around the country. Most Jewish people in Argentina are Jewish in name and heritage only, rather than being religious Jews. However, every major city has a synagogue (a Jewish place of worship), a Hebrew school, and a Jewish cemetery.

In Argentina, Jews are generally accepted in all walks of life. Therefore, the country was visibly shaken by a 1992 terrorist bombing of the Israeli Embassy in Buenos Aires. Argentines were even more distressed by the bombing of the Mutual Israeli/Argentine Association (AMAI) building in Buenos Aires on July 18, 1994. Eighty-six people died in that blast. Although no one was arrested for the crime, Middle Eastern extremists are believed to be responsible. Every Monday morning a group of people gather in front of the Palace of Justice in Buenos Aires in silent remembrance of those who were killed. They say such collective memory is one way to prevent other attacks. At a memorial service in 1997, artist Alicia Messing unveiled a sorrowful painting, *El Eco de la Memoria*, to commemorate the deaths.

Another 1.5 percent of Argentines belong to Ukrainian, Greek, and Syrian Orthodox and Armenian churches. In addition, some 300,000 Muslims follow the faith of Islam and several thousand people follow Asian religions.

Churches, convents, and shrines—old and new—are seen everywhere in Argentina. The Argentines respect such places because of their historical and religious significance and often make the sign of the cross when passing a church. The dead are not forgotten. Everyone gathers at the cemetery on the anniversary of a friend's or relative's death.

Religions of Argentina	
Roman Catholics	93.0%
Protestants	2.5%
Jews	2.0%
Orthodox Christians	1.5%
Other	1.0%

Eva Perón's tomb in Recoleta Cemetary

Sometimes, old religious sites became used for other purposes as the years passed. For example, look at Buenos Aires' upscale neighborhood of Recoleta. The area was named after an order of friars who dedicated their monastery in Recoleta to the Virgin of Pilar in 1716. Their neighbors called the priests' compound the Convento de los Padres Recoletos, or La Recoleta for short.

The monastery was closed in 1820 and the friars' orchard became the city's first official cemetery. Many famous citizens are buried there. Visitors always leave roses and lilies at the foot of Eva (Evita) Duarte Perón's tomb, where a plaque announces that she was "the champion of the working classes." Some grave sites are oddly shaped. Dr. Pedro Arata's tomb is one of the most interesting. It looks like an Egyptian pyramid. Dr. Frederico Leloir's tomb has room for sixty

The Metropolitan Cathedral

The Metropolitan Cathedral (above) is in the heart of downtown Buenos Aires. On the right side of the main entrance, a torch is always burning. This eternal flame

(left) honors General José de San Martín, Argentina's national hero. The cathedral stands on the site where the city's first chapel was built in 1585.

The ground for the cathedral was blessed and construction began on the cathedral in 1622. It took workers until 1791 to finish the structure. Interior decorating and last-minute touches continued for another thirty years.

French architects Prosper Catelin and Pierre Benoit were hired to design the cathedral portico, which is a porch of twelve pillars on the front of the building. Above the columns is a relief sculpture by Joseph Dubourdie. The scene represents the political reconciliation of Buenos Aires and the provinces after the national revolution.

The main altar (below) is one of the best examples of Spanish colonial design in South America. Inside the cathedral are the Mausoleum of San Martín and the tombs of other Argentine generals, as well as the tomb of the country's Unknown Soldier. San Martín's ashes are kept in a red marble vase at the foot of a monument dedicated to his victories. A military honor guard, the Grenaderos, is always present.

coffins. The inside dome of his mausoleum is covered with pure gold. Remedios Escaleda de San Martín, wife of the famous general, is also buried at La Recoleta.

In the old days, a small, open-topped cart pulled by black mules was used to take dead children to the cemetery. The cart was painted white, with light-blue silk curtains around the sides. It was driven by a young man dressed in scarlet with a plume of white feathers in his hat. Sometimes he drove so fast that the tiny bodies flopped around inside the cart as if they were trying to escape. Whenever youngsters saw this cart careening down their street, they ran screaming into their houses. Nobody wanted to be taken away by the scarlet coachman.

Pope John Paul II celebrates mass at a Buenos Aires Stadium.

The Roman Catholic Church does not hold as strong a position in people's lives as it did several generations ago. However, when Pope John Paul II visited Argentina in 1982 during a South American tour, interest in religion was reborn for a time. Thousands turned out to see the pope as he said mass. John Paul also met with General Leopoldo Galtieri, then the country's president.

Recoleta's Burial Traditions

In the 1820s, horse-drawn hearses went around Buenos Aires to pick up the dead. The drivers then pulled up to the front gate of the Recoleta cemetery and, inside the hearses, the corpses were taken out of the coffins. This was done so that the coffins could be used again. The bodies were dumped onto the ground for the grave diggers to pick up and bury. The bodies were laid four at a time in long, unmarked graves and piled on top of each other. Then dirt was thrown over them and tightly packed down. Thousands of poor people were buried in this way. However, wealthy businessman Facundo Quiroga asked to be buried standing up. His wishes were obeyed, so his coffin can be seen standing upright, supported by two pillars. A statue called Sorrowing Mary, supposedly representing his widow, stands guard.

Ghost Stories

Argentines in the countryside love to tell stories, especially spooky tales. It is easy to believe in ghosts when you hear the wind roar in the night and see the moon playing hide-and-seek with the clouds. On such stormy nights, the old-timers whisper, vaporlike horsemen gallop past the far-flung *estancias*, the lonely ranch houses far out on the Pampa. These silent riders are entirely wrapped in wispy gray capes that cover their faces and enfold their bodies. The only sound comes from the thundering hooves of their skeletal horses. In the bright, sunny morning, there will be no sign of their passing, not even a hoofprint. According to the storytellers, this is Death and its companions returning from doing some terrible deed far out on the plains.

Clearly, while the Argentines may not be regular churchgoers, they appreciate and respect the mysterious, religious, and spiritual side of their lives.

Land of Poets, Scholars, and Athletes

Argentine writers have always been in the forefront of South America's literary world. People from all walks of life have written books. President Domingo Faustino Sarmiento wrote a classic book called *Facundo*, about a *caudillo* (political strongman) and his family. The book is considered a masterpiece.

Jorge Luis Borges

JOSÉ HERNÁNDEZ, WHO WAS ALSO ACTIVE IN national politics, wrote *Martín Fierro*, a long poem about the gauchos. In the 1920s, a group of intense young writers called themselves the "Martinfierristas," after Hernández's hero. A well-known member of this informal club was Jorge Luis Borges—a poet who was nominated several times for the Nobel Prize in literature. By the mid-1980s, Borges had become a crusty conservative, but he was still a literary lion who was always considered one of South America's greatest poets.

Argentine Writers

The list of Argentine writers could go on almost forever. There's Eduardo Mallea, Ricardo Guiradles, Ezequiel Martinez Estrada, Conrade Nale Roxlo, Macendonio Fernández, Ernesto Sabato, and dozens of others. Manuel Puig's novel *Kiss of the Spider Woman* was made into an award-winning movie. Victoria O'Campo spent a fortune publishing *Sur*, whose pages were filled with thrilling stories and poems by Argentine authors. She also supported the work of writers from around the world. For years, *Sur* was considered one of the world's best literary magazines.

Opposite: **A newsstand near Plaza General Martín in Buenos Aires**

Argentina has at least 8,000 bookstores and many are open twenty-four hours a day. A major book fair is held annually in Buenos Aires, and a recent exhibition attracted 700,000 visitors. Argentina's 200 publishers produce an astounding 21 million books a year, exporting 50 percent of them throughout South America. Publishing is one of Argentina's largest industries. Of course, many books sell only 5,000 copies or so, but the figures are still remarkable. The National Library in Buenos Aires, founded in 1810, is one of the largest in the Americas. Some of its rare books date back to the 1400s.

And if Argentines still don't have enough to read, Buenos Aires boasts of twelve daily newspapers and fifty magazines. Generally there is press freedom in the country. But in the 1990s, investigative journalists got into trouble for writing about links between top government officials and drug dealers. The case of reporter José Luis Cabezas, who was tortured and murdered in 1997, was one of about 800 reported attacks on media personnel during that time. Amnesty International and the Freedom Forum, which monitor such incidents, have called journalism one of Argentina's most dangerous professions. Yet editors and reporters bravely agree that it is important to hold government accountable, thereby preserving freedom.

Intellectuals are among the most prominent figures in South America, and Argentina is no exception. Because of their education and their eloquence, the country's literary and artistic figures are admired by both the rich and poor. Sometimes this has gotten them into trouble with the government, especially during the years of the military control. But they carried on. The week after the Falklands War ended, *Los Pychi Ciegos (The Blind Armadillos)* was published. Author Rodolfo Fogwill wrote about a group of captured Argentine conscripts who end up working for the victorious British troops in exchange for food.

The Tango

Many countries have national dances. Chile has the quecha, Ireland has the jig, Scotland has the Highland fling, the United States has the square dance, and Argentina has the tango.

A couple dancing the tango

Street musicians in Buenos Aires

The tango evolved from many musical forms, basically from the polka and a Spanish dance called the *habanera*. The music of black freedmen who lived in the Río de la Plata area was also an influence. By the end of the 1800s, today's classical tango was recognizable.

At first, it was the music of the gauchos and the lower classes. But in the 1920s, Europeans fell in love with its rhythm and its sensuality. Upper-class Argentines began dancing the tango. The bandoneon, a cross between an accordion and a concertina, is the primary instrument in tango music. The bandoneon was brought to Argentina by German sailors. Violins, guitars, and other instruments can be included as backup. Tango clubs along Buenos Aires' Avenida Corriente are always crowded. Casa Blanca and Club del Vino are among the best known.

There have been many tango composers, including Francisco Canaro, who introduced the tango to Japan. Astor Piazolla is an internationally famous bandoneon player who has written scores for films. He also composed a ballet score for Moscow's Bolshoi Theater. A famous tango singer, Carlos Gardel, died years ago, but his records are still popular. His gravesite in La Chararita cemetery is regularly visited by tango fans who say that "Gardel sings better every day," meaning that nobody has ever been as good as Gardel. A well-known contemporary tango singer is Edmundo Leonel Rivero, who owns the trendy Viejo Almacén nightclub in Buenos Aires.

Music and Dance

Argentines love all kinds of music. The first missionaries stressed the importance of learning music and taught classes in their frontier schools. Amancio Alcorta (1805–1862) is considered the first native Argentine classical composer and many others have followed in his footsteps. Pop musical compositions were written by Felipe Boero, Pascual de Rogatis, Alberto Williams, Carlos Guastavino, and Alberto Ginastera. Noted orchestra leaders have included Mariano Drago and Juan José Castro.

Colón Opera Theater at night

Next to the tango, opera must be the most popular music in Argentina, a tribute to the country's Italian heritage. It's not uncommon to hear street musicians singing beautiful arias. Fifty Argentine operas have been introduced in this country and more than twenty were first produced abroad. The operas of Arturo Beruti (1862–1938) are known around the world. As early as 1825, operas were staged in Buenos Aires.

Ballet seems to have captured the fancy of Argentines, just as the tango did. The names of Argentinita, Liliama Belfiore, Olga Ferri, Norma Fontenla, José Neglia, and Iris Scaccheri recall images of their grace and composure on the stage. Choreographer Oscar Araiz is said to have directed some of the best dances ever presented in South America.

Argentina has a thriving music industry.

Rock Groups, Theater, and Film

Wild and upbeat Argentine rock bands are known throughout South America. Young fans flock to hear Enanitos Verdes, Soda Stereo, the Sacados, Sui Generis, Los Abuelos de la Nada, Ladrones Sueltos, Los Fabulosos Cadillacs, and Fito Páez wherever they perform. They take rhythms from many cultures and turn them into a distinctive Argentine sound. Music stores do a booming business with CDs and tapes of both homegrown and international talent. Local balladeer Leon Gieco's song *"Solo le Pido a Dios"* ("I Only Ask God") became a popular antiwar song during the Falklands War.

Argentine playwrights have been writing since colonial days. *Siripo*, written by Manuel de Lavarden in the late 1700s, is thought to be among the first plays written by a native Argentine. In 1901, Enrique Garcia Vallosa thrilled theater-goers in South America and Europe with his dramatic long play *Jesus Nazareno*. Roberto Payro is known for social commentary in his plays that criticize the wealthy, old-time landowners and their free-spending lifestyles.

There are more than 300 theaters in Buenos Aires alone, plus several hundred regional and community theaters. Many social and sports clubs have halls for staging amateur productions. Argentine actors and actresses Elsa O'Connor, Mecha Ortiz, Lea Conti, Osvaldo Terranova, Sergio Renan, Pepe Soriano, and Alfredo Alcon have been among the most popular stage performers.

Art in Argentina

There are more than 100 art galleries in Buenos Aires and hundreds more around the countryside. Yet painting, sculpture, photography, and the other visual arts in Argentina have only recently been recognized for their quality. Each year, at least 6,000 art shows are held in the Argentine capital. That doesn't include the many galleries that present exhibitions in other cities. In addition, every year, art galleries from around

The Argentine Film Industry

The Twelfth Annual Festival Internacional de Cine De Mar Del Plata is one of the world's best-known film festivals. It began in 1954 and was attended by many famous movie stars. Throughout the years, it has attracted top international cinema talents. Despite its success, however, the military governments of the 1970s and 1980s canceled the festival because of political disagreements. The event made a comeback in November 1996, in conjunction with the founding of the Argentine Cinema Foundation.

The 1996 festival winner was Argentine-born Alejandro Agresti. His film *Buenos Aires Viceversa* dealt with two teenagers trying to find their parents who disappeared during Argentina's Dirty War. Agresti started making movies in the late 1970s and has become a noted film celebrity. Most of his raw, earthy movies depict life in the hustle-bustle of modern Argentina.

Other noted Argentine directors include Hector Olivera, whose *The Night of the Pencils* told the true story of six high-school friends kidnapped and tortured during the Dirty War. Luis Puenzo directed *The Official Story* (above), another chilling story of the war. In the film the Argentine upper classes are condemned for believing only what the government tells them. From these stories, it is easy to see how deeply that era affected the Argentine consciousness.

the world contribute pieces for a "Gallery of the Galleries" exhibition in Buenos Aires.

In colonial times, most of the art dealt with religious themes. It wasn't until the 1830s, when Carlos Morel and Fernando García Molina began exhibiting, that native Argentine artists became well known.

In 1896, the opening of the National Museum of Fine Arts gave a big boost to Argentine art. At last, the nation's artists had a place of national stature in which to exhibit. Soon, the names of Argentines became world famous. Quinquela Martin painted scenes from the docks in

National Museum of Fine Arts

Buenos Aires. Pedro Figari enjoyed painting about long-ago city life. Sculptors such as Lucio Fontana and Fernando Arranz are among the many artists who work in marble, ceramics, and clay.

Fútbol Fans

Few countries love *fútbol* (football, or soccer) as much as Argentina does. The British brought the sport to South America in the 1800s and soon everyone was playing. Argentine teams are noted for their finesse in handling the ball. They are very emotional but skilled players who attack and defend with equal ease. The top players are often featured in newspapers and sports magazines.

The Argentines captured the World Cup championship in 1978 in front of a delighted crowd in Buenos Aires, rolling over the world's most powerful soccer teams. The stands went crazy when team captain Daniel Pasarella ran around the field with the huge trophy after the final game. He and his teammates were national heroes.

In 1979, an Argentine team won the Junior World Championship, which was played in Japan. At the height of the 1982 Falklands War, both England and Argentina competed in the World Cup games in Madrid, Spain, while hundreds of millions of people from around the world watched on television. But the two teams never met on the field because both were edged out in the quarterfinals. For a time, the games gave the people of both nations something to think about besides the harsh war in the Atlantic. The finals were eventually won by Italy, who defeated the Germans. Argentines of Italian descent cheered and applauded their ancestral country.

In 1997, the Argentine youth team reconfirmed its championship status in the under-twenty group by again capturing the FIFA/Coca-Cola World Cup. This is the world's premier competition for younger players. The Argentines, coached by José Nestor Pekerman, defeated the tough Brazilians in the quarterfinals and the Irish in the semifinals. In its final match, Argentina smashed Uruguay with a 2 to 1 score and won the prize.

Argentina was disappointed in the 1996 Olympics in Atlanta, Georgia, when its football team was narrowly defeated, 3–2, by the hard-as-nails Nigerians. At first, Argentina's hopes soared when Claudio Lopez slammed a header goal in the early minutes of the match. But the Argentines flagged under the powerful attack of the African team. The Olympics are the only large international football competition in which Argentina has competed but never won. In 1928, it lost its only other Olympic bid for the gold medal in football.

Soccer is one of Argentina's favorite sports.

Diego Maradona

Diego Maradona was one of the greatest footballers in history. He was born on October 30, 1960, in the Vila Fiorito on the outskirts of Buenos Aires. He started with the Argentinos Juniors, moved up to the Boca Juniors, and went on to play for the Argentine national team and in Spain. Maradona played in four World Cup championships: Spain, 1982; Mexico, 1986; Italy, 1990; and the United States, 1994. Fans remember his famous goal in the Mexican games in which he outdribbled nine English players and the goalkeeper.

In 1984, he moved to Naples, Italy, and helped them win their two Italian championships, a Coppa Italia, and other major victories. In the 1994 World Cup, however, Maradona was tested for drugs after a game against Nigeria and was found to have used an illegal substance. As punishment, he was suspended from playing soccer for a year. Maradona eventually returned to the game, much to the delight of his fans.

Auto Racers and Pato Players

Professional auto racing seems to come naturally for some Argentines. Since the 1950s, they have burned up the tracks in a dozen countries. Juan Manuel Fangio was world champion driver five times. Carlos Alberto Reutemann has been a top-notch Grand Prix contestant. Ricardo Zunino was another formidable driver with nerves of steel. The challenging Buenos Aires track always brings in top competitors from around the world. They drive sporty Ferraris, Renaults, Hondas, Peugeots, and Mercedes Benz race cars. The Argentine course is considered one of the toughest in the world, with seventeen hair-raising corners and plenty of opportunities to spin out of control.

Horsepower of another sort is seen in the rough-and-tumble game of pato, which originated with the gauchos. In the old days, a live duck (*pato* in Spanish) was stuffed into a sack with only its head sticking out. Two teams on horseback fought over the sack, racing back and forth over a 3-mile (5-km)-long field.

The game often degenerated into a bloody brawl and was banned in 1822. However, it soon reappeared under the administration of President Juan Manuel de Rosas, who was a fan of anything connected with gauchos. The Argentine Pato Federation was founded in 1941, with forty participating clubs. It is less savage now because a large ball is used instead of a helpless, terrified duck. The game is similar to polo, which is also popular in Argentina—thanks to the British settlers. The players in pato, however, grab the ball with their hands instead of hitting it with a mallet as in polo. They then try to stuff the ball into a large net, in order to score.

Fun and Games

Since the 1940s, Argentine polo teams have won many gold medals in Olympic Games, as well as numerous other awards for their spirited play. In the 1996 Olympic Games in Atlanta, Georgia, the Argentine jumping team was one of the seventeen top finalists in this rugged horsemanship event. The gaucho and Native American tradition of fine riding is still evident.

Argentine boxers are well known in the sports world. A major fighter in the 1920s was Luis Angel Firpo—nicknamed "the Wild Bull of the Pampas." His best-known fight was in

Firpo and Dempsey in the ring before their fight

1923, when he knocked world heavyweight champion Jack Dempsey out of the ring. Dempsey, of the United States, came back to win the match.

Unfortunately, Firpo was never able to gain the heavyweight crown, but eight other Argentines have been world champions in various weight classes since then. Carlos Monzón was middleweight champ from 1970 to 1977, undefeated in fourteen challenges to his crown.

There are many other sports heroes in Argentina. The country's ice-hockey team was world champion in 1978 and many records in swimming have also been set by Argentines. Golfer Roberto De Vicenzo, marathon runners Juan Carlos Zabala and Delfo Cabrera, and tennis players Guillermo Vilas, José Luis Clerc, and Ivanna Madruga are highly respected.

Noted Triathletes

Argentines are noted triathletes. These competitions test endurance and athletic discipline in swimming, cycling, and running. In the 1996 Iron Man competition in Maui, Hawaii, accountant Mario M. Palin and student Leandro Roman were among twelve Argentines who finished near the top of the field. In 1995, Argentina's Oscar Galindez took the gold medal in the first ITU World Championship Dualthon, beating a strong international field in biking and swimming.

Café Culture

Argentina is a café society. Townspeople enjoy sitting at a sidewalk table, sipping sodas or coffee and watching the passersby. A favorite café game is chess. From the cafés, Argentine chess players have moved out to challenge the best players of other countries. Many of the better players are young people. Oscar Panno was juvenile world champion in 1952, Carlos Bielicki was juvenile world champion in 1957, and Marcelo Tempone was world cadet champion in 1979.

Chess is often played in cafés of Argentina.

The Day Off

Ramón Diaz de Amicis was happy. School was out for the summer and he had no place in particular to go that afternoon. He had spent the morning cleaning vegetables and sweeping floors at his parents' cantina, a small restaurant in Buenos Aires. Now he headed down to the wharves along the *Riachueleo* (Little River) to watch the freighters churning toward the port.

THE JANUARY SUN WAS HOT, REFLECTing back from the tin-roofed buildings. A few screeching gulls drifted on the breeze as the Riachueleo flowed into the black waters of the Río de La Plata. From several blocks away, the boy could smell the water—a mixture of dead fish, spilled diesel fuel, and rotting vegetation. But he was used to it and it didn't bother him at all.

Ramón's mom and dad operated their small restaurant on Calle Necochea in the *barrio* (neighborhood) of La Boca, not far from the docks. It had fourteen tables in the main room, a small bar, and a party room for six persons to the left of the entrance. It was not very big, but bigger than most others in the neighborhood. And a tango singer came in on weekends! Ramón thought the food his mom prepared was great, certainly better than the Gran Café Tortoni on the Avenida de Mayo or Il Piccolo Vapore or Spaddevecchio—two La Boca neighbors where the tour groups always went.

Tin-roofed houses

Opposite: **A small restaurant in Buenos Aires**

His dad, Maurice, wanted Ramón to wash dishes in the restaurant that evening. But he had three hours of freedom! And Ramón didn't mind working for his folks. It always gave him the chance to sneak an extra *empanada*. He loved the little pies stuffed with vegetables, beef, and cheese. These were also really popular with the sailors who dropped by the cantina for snacks on the way back to their ships.

Ramón loved the smells of food cooking. Jeannette, his mother, was an excellent chef. Even tourists from Brazil, Germany, and England who wandered into the cantina said so. Once, it was said, their place was written up in a guidebook.

Empanadas

Ramón had never seen a copy of the story but when visitors to the family-run restaurant asked for *locro*, the house specialty, he knew that word was getting around somehow. Locro is a thick corn stew overflowing with spicy home-made sausage, pumpkin, white beans, chunks of beef, and herbs. Ramón's mom never told anyone her secret recipe. Even his dad said he didn't dare ask. Ramón thought that was funny. His father was a tank gunner who won medals in the Falklands War and was usually not afraid of anything.

Opposite: **A menu outside a family-owned restaurant**

Maurice de Amicis always stood at the restaurant door to greet guests and show them to their tables. The family was really proud of the cantina. Visitors barely sat down for a cup of heavy coffee before the complimentary sweets, cloth napkins, and toothpicks were laid out on the red checkered tablecloth. Ramón's dad always made sure that Pepé, Hans, and Alberto, the waiters, were in top form with their white jackets clean and pressed. Regulars returned to their restaurant because of the delicious food and the fine service. Actors, journalists, and writers often came by for supper. They almost took over the place for the entire night when they arrived to eat. The happy crowd would sing and dance the tarantella, a fast, whirling Italian folk dance. By the time the diners had finished some delicious *arroz con leche* (rice pudding), they were ready to burst. At least that's what the film critic from *La Nacion* (*The Nation*) newspaper told Ramón with a satisfied grin one time.

National Holidays in Argentina	
New Year's Day	January 1
Good Friday	Friday before Easter
Easter	movable Sunday in March or April
Labor Day	May 1
May 25	Anniversary of the Revolution
Malvina Day	Monday closest to June 10
Flag Day	Monday closest to June 20
Independence Day	July 9
Anniversary of the death of General José de San Martín	August 17
Columbus Day	October 12
Christmas Day	December 25

Argentine Cuisine

There is no need to go hungry in Argentina. The country, however, is often considered a vegetarian's nightmare because meat tops the menu everywhere. Beef is a dietary staple on the Pampa—the home of the large cattle ranches—as well as throughout the country. Argentine beef is prized for its healthy, low-cholesterol quality. Special cuts, such as the *tira de asado* (crosscut ribs) and *matambre* (cuts between the ribs and haunches) are particularly prized. Sausages made from beef are delicious. The wide variety includes *chorizos* (red sausages), *morcillas* (black pudding), and *salchica* (a long sausage). The meat is often seasoned with hot chimichurri or criolla sauce.

In the Patagonian Andes, San Carlos de Bariloche is known for its fabulous dishes, especially *curantos* (a mixture of shellfish, meat, and vegetables cooked on hot stones). The city is also famous for chocolate fondues, with more than 130 varieties to choose from.

In Misiones and Formosa, a popular dish is *locro norteno*, made with beef, pumpkin, and cassava, a heavy root plant like a sweet potato. The mbeyú is a fried cake originally made by the Guaraní tribe with tapioca, milk, salt, and cheese. The *chipa* is a cake built up with the same ingredients, along with eggs. Don't let the words "Paraguayan soup" fool you. It is a bread made with white corn floor, cheese, onion, and spices.

And don't forget a mouth-watering dessert! Cookies called *alfajores* are filled with *dulce de leche* (caramel sauce) and covered with rich vanilla or chocolate. They are found in the popular resort community of Córdoba and are often taken home as presents or as a sweet reminder of vacation. Tea cakes crammed with raisins, walnuts, orange peel, brown sugar, and cinnamon are popular around the old Welsh settlements near the Chubut River.

Life in La Boca

When the newspaper reporter heard that Ramón collected stamps and liked movies, he sent over a set of Argentine seventy-five-centavos stamps that depicted the 100th anniversary of cinema. Ramón especially liked the one showing a scene from Charlie Chaplin's 1952 film, *Limelight*.

When Ramón got older, he would also wait on tables and meet famous Argentines who often came to La Boca for the restaurants and nightlife. Until he could work the tables, Ramón's job was to clear the tables, carry the dishes and utensils away, and wash them in the kitchen. When his folks retired,

La Boca district of Buenos Aires

he would run the restaurant. He thought of maybe going to cooking school after high school. But his mom was the best teacher and he was already learning about herbs and spices.

Ramón loved living in La Boca, one of the oldest areas of Buenos Aires. One of his history books said that it was the site of the original city when it was called *Nuestra Señora de Buenos Aires* (Our Lady of Fair Winds). Explorer Pedro de Mendoza supposedly set up his flag somewhere in Ramón's neighborhood in 1536. Of course, the area looked very different back then. It was on a floodplain and the settlers had to build their houses on pilings so they would not be washed away.

The Avellaneda Bridge

Ramón's great-grandfather, Rudolpho Amicis, was one of the thousands of Italian immigrants who settled there in the 1880s. He came aboard a transatlantic steamer called the *Galileo,* from his home port of Genoa. After he arrived in Argentina, he worked for years in a warehouse. Hanging in Ramón's living room was a faded portrait of his great-grandfather—an elderly man with a large mustache, surrounded by his family. Ramón's father was also in the picture, as a baby being held by an aunt. On his mom's side, Ramón had more Italian blood, as well as Greek. It was hard to trace all the connections because much of her family had been in Argentina since before the country gained independence.

After leaving the restaurant when his morning chores were finished, Ramón wanted to get a good view of the neighborhood. So he stopped at the Avellaneda Bridge, which spans the Riachueleo at Avenida Almirante Brown. Because the escalators to the top-level pedestrian walkway were not working, he ran up the four flights of stairs to the highest point on the bridge. From there, he took a quick look around.

Near the bridge, billionaire shipping tycoon Aristotle Onassis used to work as a ferryman when he first immigrated to Argentina. Onassis eventually married Jacqueline Kennedy, widow of U.S. president John F. Kennedy. Folks in La Boca still remembered Onassis, one of the neighborhood's best-known former residents. When he was on top of the bridge, Ramón often wondered what it would be like to be a billionaire. But up there he felt as if he was already at the top of the world.

Family and Familiar Places

From his vantage point, Ramón spotted some friends kicking a football. He scampered down from the bridge to join them. Many painters lived on the street and they were getting ready for that Saturday's art fair, so the boys were careful not to get in their way. After some fancy dribbling, Ramón moved on. He followed the turn of the road fronting the river and came

Córdoba is Argentina's second-largest city.

to Vuelta de Rocha, a small square. Ramón looked at the monument there—a mast, rudder, and anchor standing in a rock mound. The sculpture paid homage to sailors lost at sea. One of Ramón's great-uncles died in an Atlantic storm years ago when his freighter sank, so Ramón blessed himself and said a little prayer.

By then it was time to head back to the restaurant. The shadows were already starting to creep along the streets.

Ramón ran past the Santuario de Nuestra Senora Madre de los Immigrantes, the small church on Necochea Street. Every Sunday, he and his family went to mass there. The church was built in 1967 to honor the immigrants from other countries who settled in La Boca. His dad and mom always told him to pray for great-grandpa Amicis and all the people who came with him to Argentina.

When he dashed through the back door of the cantina, his mother waved a spoon at him. It was coated with delicious tomato sauce. "We just talked with Uncle Felipé in Córdoba. He hopes you can visit your cousins in February before school starts. They plan on going fishing and hiking," she said, between stirring more sauce on the giant stove. "Your father and I decided you can go if you do an especially good job on the dishes for the next few weeks." That was an easy promise for Ramón to make.

Ramón was excited. He was old enough to take the train from Buenos Aires to Córdoba and would then be picked up by car at the station. From there, his uncle would take him to his estancia in the valley of La Punilla, north of the city. His cousins, María, Juan, Jean, and Martín, were all about the same age as Ramón and so they always had a good time together. Uncle Felipé raised cattle on the Pampa, just like the gauchos of the old days. He often came to Buenos Aires on business. Sometimes, the cousins came along and Ramón showed them around his neighborhood. But unlike Ramón's small house in the city, their rambling ranch home was filled with saddles, spurs, and other riding gear. It was a great place to visit.

Life on the Estancia

Uncle Felipé, his father's oldest brother, started working as a ranch hand in Córdoba province years ago. By carefully saving, he was able to earn enough to buy his small estancia in the heart of Argentina's fertile "breadbasket." Ramón's Aunt Estelle was a mixture of Welsh, Quechau Indian, and German. She and Felipé met when attending business classes at the university in

A gaucho driving cattle

Córdoba. Her family had raised sheep in Patagonia's Chubut province since the 1870s, so she was used to farm life and helped Felipé manage their estancia. Aunt Estelle always told silly jokes. When Ramón was just a little kid, she told a funny story about a Patagonian chicken that lost its feathers in a fierce gale. Its owner had to knit a sweater to keep the bird warm. At the time, Ramón believed her. He was older and wiser now but he still laughed at her jokes. No matter how busy she was, she always took time for tea late in the afternoon. That was part of her Welsh heritage, she told Ramón.

That evening during work, Ramón kept thinking of what he should pack for the trip. Jeans were at the top of his list because there would be the chance to ride a horse, not something that many children in La Boca would ever do. All his cousins had their own horses. They were really lucky. Of course, he would also bring his bathing suit because there was a natural pool at the estancia where everybody just jumped in and splashed around. He figured he should bring an extra pair of sneakers too and probably a sweatshirt—and his football, of course, because Cousin Martín played goalie on his school team. "I'll have to show him how the city guys can play," Ramón said out loud. Luckily no one heard him above the din of clashing pots and pans in the kitchen.

Day's End

After work, Ramón raced home and started gathering everything he might need for the trip even though it was days away. He was really tired, but he turned on the radio to catch the latest football scores. Whenever he wanted to watch a match on television, he had to go to a friend's house because the Amicis family did not have a TV set. That night, Ramón especially wanted to hear the latest about the Boca Juniors. That was the club where his hero Diego Maradona used to play. But soon his eyelids were really heavy. Even listening to the roundup of the latest matches wasn't enough to keep him awake for long.

As Ramón drifted off to sleep, he could hardly wait for the stories he could tell when classes started again!

Timeline

Argentine History

Juan Díaz de Solís sails up Río de la Plata and is killed by Indians.	1516
Magellan lands in Patagonia.	1520
Pedro de Mendoza builds a fort called Buenos Aires.	1536
Spanish settlers from Peru establish Santiago del Estero, the first permanent town in Argentina.	1553
Argentina and Great Britain dispute ownership of the Falkland Islands.	1776–1777
Viceroyalty of the Río de la Plata establishes a seat of power in Buenos Aires.	1776
Argentina declares its independence.	1810
José de San Martín becomes Argentine army commander.	1814

World History

c. 2500 B.C.	Egyptians build the pyramids and Sphinx in Giza.
563 B.C.	Buddha is born in India.
A.D. 313	The Roman emperor Constantine recognizes Christianity.
610	The prophet Muhammad begins preaching a new religion called Islam.
1054	The Eastern (Orthodox) and Western (Roman) churches break apart.
1066	William the Conqueror defeats the English in the Battle of Hastings.
1095	Pope Urban II proclaims the First Crusade.
1215	King John seals the Magna Carta.
1300s	The Renaissance begins in Italy.
1347	The Black Death sweeps through Europe.
1453	Ottoman Turks capture Constantinople, conquering the Byzantine Empire.
1492	Columbus arrives in North America.
1500s	The Reformation leads to the birth of Protestantism.
1776	The Declaration of Independence is signed.
1789	The French Revolution begins.

Argentine History		World History	
Argentine government claims Falklands (Malvinas).	1820		
Argentina is rocked by a civil war.	1828–1829		
Great Britain retakes the Falklands (Malvinas).	1833		
Argentina's constitution is approved.	1853		
Buenos Aires is declared Argentina's capital.	1862		
		1865	The American Civil War ends.
		1914	World War I breaks out.
		1917	The Bolshevik Revolution brings Communism to Russia.
The Argentine economy is battered by a worldwide economic depression.	1929–1937	1929	Worldwide economic depression begins.
The military, led by General José F. Uriburu, takes control of the government.	1930		
World War II starts; Argentina is neutral, but the military supports both Germany and Italy.	1939	1939	World War II begins, following the German invasion of Poland.
Juan Perón is named vice president.	1944		
Perón is president of Argentina.	1946–1955		
Military coup overthrows Perón.	1955		
		1957	The Vietnam War starts.
Perón returns to Argentina and is reelected president.	1973		
Perón dies and his widow, Isabel Perón, is named president; a military coup deposes Señora Perón.	1974		
Argentina and Great Britain wage war over the Falkland Islands.	1982		
Dr. Raúl Alfonsín becomes the first civilian president since the 1976 coup.	1982		
Alfonsín relinquishes leadership to Carlos Menem.	1989	1989	The Berlin Wall is torn down, as communism crumbles in Eastern Europe.
Menem becomes the first Argentine president in more than 40 years to win consecutive terms.	1995	1996	Bill Clinton reelected U.S. president.

Fast Facts

Official name: *República Argentine* (Argentine Republic)

Capital: Buenos Aires

An assistant at a polo match

Perito Moreno

Official language:	Spanish	
Official religion:	Roman Catholicism	
National anthem:	*Himno Nacional Argentino* (Argentine National Anthem)	
Government:	Federal republic with two legislative houses (the Senate and the House of Deputies)	
Chief of state and head of government:	President	
Area:	1,073,400 square miles (2,780,092 sq km)	
Dimensions:	North-south, 2,300 miles (3,700 km) East-west, 980 miles (1,577 km)	
Coordinates for geographic center:	34° 00' S, 64° 00' W	
Bordering countries:	Argentina shares 517 miles (832 km) with Bolivia; 760 miles (1,224 km) with Brazil; 3,198 miles (5,150 km) with Chile; 1,167 miles (1,880 km) with Paraguay; and 360 miles (579 km) with Uruguay.	
Highest elevation:	Aconcagua, 22,834 feet (6,960 m) above sea level	
Lowest elevation:	Valdés Peninsula, 131 feet (40 m) below sea level	

Average temperatures:

	In northern Argentina	In southern Argentina
January:	80°F (27°C)	60°F (16°C)
August:	60°F (16°C)	32°F (0°C)

Average annual rainfall:

Mesopotamia
more than 60 inches (150 cm)

Piedmont and Patagonia
less than 10 inches (25 cm)

National population (1996): 34,995,000

Population of largest cities in Argentina (1996):

Buenos Aires	2,960,976
(Greater Buenos Aires)	12,582,321
Córdoba	1,208,713
Rosario	1,078,374
La Plata	542,567

Famous Landmarks:

▶ *Casa Rosada* (Buenos Aires)

▶ *Plaza de Mayo* (Buenos Aires)

▶ *Metropolitan Cathedral* (Buenos Aires)

▶ *Recoleta Cemetery* (Buenos Aires)

▶ *Iguaçú Falls* (on the Argentina-Brazil border)

Iguaçú Falls

Industry: Service industries and manufacturing account for most of Argentina's gross domestic product (GDP). Argentina's fertile farmland, however, is the country's most important natural resource and forms the basis of the economy. Argentine factories process farm products, primarily beef, wool, and hides. Additionally, much of Argentina's service industries depend upon agriculture, including transportation and banking.

Argentina's factories produce most of the nation's consumer goods, including food, clothing, and household equipment. It imports much of the heavy machinery and other goods needed for production.

Currency: Argentina's basic unit of currency is the *peso*. 1998 exchange rate: Arg$1.00=U.S.$1.00

Weights and measures:	Metric system	
Literacy:	96.2%	
Common words and phrases:	*Buenos días*	Good morning
	Buenas tardes	Good afternoon
	Buenas noches	Good night
	Hasta la vista	See you again
	¿Cómo está usted?	How are you?
	¿Bien, gracias. Y usted?	Fine, thanks. And you?
	Feliz Navidad	Merry Christmas
	Lo siento	I'm sorry
	Habla más despacio, por favor.	Please speak more slowly.
	¿Qué hora es?	What time is it?

The Metropolitan Cathedral

Famous People:

Jorge Luis Borges (1899–1986)
Author

Juan Manuel Fangio (1911–1995)
Grand Prix race car driver

Diego Maradona (1960–)
Soccer player

Carlos Saúl Menem (1930–)
Argentine president

Juan Perón (1895–1974)
Argentine president

María Estela (Isabel) Martínez de Perón (1931–)
Argentine president

María Eva (Evita) Duarte Perón (1919–1952)
Argentine First Lady and political figure

Manuel Puig (1932–1990)
Writer

To Find Out More

Nonfiction

▶ Egan, E. W. *Argentina in Pictures*. Minneapolis: Lerner, 1994

▶ Gofen, Ethel. *Argentina*, 2nd ed. Tarrytown, N.Y.: Marshall Cavendish, 1991.

▶ Liebowitz, Sol. *Argentina*. New York: Chelsea House, 1990.

▶ Peterson, Marge, and Rob Peterson. *Argentina: A Wild West Heritage*, 2nd ed. New York: Dillon Press, 1996.

Biography

▶ Brusca, María Cristina. *On the Pampas*. New York: Henry Holt, 1991.

▶ Brusca, María Cristina. *My Mama's Little Ranch on the Pampas*. New York: Henry Holt, 1994.

Fiction

▶ Kalnay, Francis. *Chucaro: Wild Pony of the Pampa*. New York: Walker & Co., 1993.

▶ Slaughter, Charles H. *The Dirty War: A Novel*. New York: Walker and Co., 1994.

Folktales

▶ Van Laan, Nancy. Illustrated by Beatrice Vidal. *The Magic Bean Tree: A Legend from Argentina*. Boston: Houghton Mifflin Co., 1998.

Websites

▶ **Consulate of Argentina, Toronto, Canada**
http://www.consargtoro.org/
Contains pictures of Argentina, links to other sites about the country, and travel and trade information.

▶ **Consulate General of the Republic of Argentina in Chicago**
http://www.uic.edu/orgs/argentina/
Provides information about trade and travel between the United States and Argentina as well as cultural links.

▶ **CIA World Fact Book**
http://www.odci.gov/cia/
publications/factbook/
country-frame.html
Up-to-date geographic, economic, government, and social information about Argentina.

Organizations and Embassies

▶ **Embassy of the Argentine Republic**
1600 New Hampshire Avenue, N.W.
Washington, DC 20009
(202) 939-6400

▶ **Consulate General of the Argentine Republic**
12 West 56th Street
New York, NY 10019
(212) 603-0400

▶ **Argentina Government Tourist Office**
12 West 56th Street
New York, NY 10019
(212) 603-0443

Index

Page numbers in *italics* indicate illustrations

Meet the Author

Martin Hintz is a member of the Society of American Travel Writers, with hundreds of magazine and newspaper articles to his credit. A former newspaper reporter, he is the author of *Poland* and *Haiti* in the Enchantment of the World series and a number of books in the America the Beautiful series.

Being a writer involves getting out and experiencing the world. Hintz's travels have taken him to the top of the Swiss Alps and to below sea level at the Dead Sea. He has tracked wolves in northern Wisconsin and looked for wild boar in the jungles of the Bahamas. He sipped tea in Jaffa and soda in Helsinki; he sailed in the Caribbean and rode horseback in New Brunswick. From all this, he has written more than fifty books and contributed stories and chapters to numerous others.

Not all of Hintz's writing deals with travel. He has written two books on the circus, including one on how to train ele-

phants, a book about computers, a cookbook, four books on drag racing, four holiday books, and one book on Irish wit and wisdom. The latter was easy. He is the publisher of *The Irish American Post,* a bimonthly news magazine. Hintz recently walked 300 miles and wore out a pair of boots researching a guidebook on hiking in Wisconsin.

To write *Argentina,* Hintz conducted extensive interviews with political, cultural, educational, and business leaders in the country, as well as with students and ordinary people. In addition to library research and a great deal of reading, he also used resources found on the World Wide Web. On the Internet, he discovered all sorts of up-to-date, helpful material. He now knows where to take tango lessons in Buenos Aires and can find the country's average temperature.

Photo Credits

Photographs ©:

Allsport USA: 111 (David Leah), 112 (Billy Strickland)

AP/Wide World Photos: 55 (Lucio Solari), 52 top

Archive Photos: 49 bottom, 101

Art Resource: 39 top

Carlos Goldin: 91

Chip and Rosa Maria de la Cueva Peterson: 19, 29, 73 bottom, 78, 85, 97 bottom left, 116, 119

Corbis-Bettmann: 41, 43 top, 46, 47, 92

D. Donne Bryant Stock Photography: 23 (Botti/L.S.), 20, 87, 105 (Carlos Goldin), 17 top (Lina Jovanovich), 27 (Peter Lang/The Photoworks), 54, 97 top, 133 (Chris R. Sharp), 64 (Caica Souto)

Gamma-Liaison: 77 bottom, 90 (Giulio Andreini), 57, 68 top (Gary Payne)

International Stock Photo: 37, 25 (Aldo Sessa-Buenos Aires), 100 (Chad Ehlers)

Kobal Collection: 108

Larry Luxner: 18, 21 top, 26, 68 bottom, 69, 70, 71, 72, 75, 80 bottom, 83, 89, 97 bottom right, 106, 109, 115, 120, 122, 124, 132 bottom

Magnum Photos: 15 top (Stuart Franklin), 117

Monkmeyer Press: 12 (Arlene Collins), 118 (Lew Merrim), 24 (Podesta), 126 (Sanguinetti)

National Geographic Image Collection: 32, 65, 77 top (James P. Blair), 17 bottom (O. Louis Mazzatenta)

North Wind Picture Archives: 38, 39 bottom, 43 bottom, 79, 80 top

Robert Fried: 2, 7 top, 8, 14 bottom, 21 bottom, 22 center, 58, 59, 82, 84, 94, 104, 121, 132 top

Superstock, Inc.: 45 (Musee Nat du Chateau de Malmaison, Rueil-Malmaison/Lauros-Giraudon, Paris)

Sygma: 60 top (C. Carrion), 53 (J.C. Criton), 98 (G. Giansanti), 52 bottom, 66 top (Diego Goldberg), 50

The Image Works: 76, 130 left (D. Boroughs), 30, 36 (Rafael Buding), 96 (M. Everton), 9, 66 bottom (Joan C. Franceschini)

Tony Stone Images: 22 top (Tim Davis), 31 (Jeanne Drake), 60 bottom (Hulton Getty), 13, 103, 131 (Robert Van Der Hils), spine (Renee Lynn), cover, back cover, 6 (David Myers), 15 bottom (Hans Strand), 7 bottom, 35 (Kim Westerskov)

UPI/Corbis-Bettmann: 48, 49 top, 51, 61, 114

Valan Photos: 22 bottom, 28 (Jean-Marie), 33, 34 (Aubrey Lang), 73 top (Y.R. Tymsira), 14 top (Wouterloot-Gregoire).

Maps by Joe LeMonnier